The Backpack Guide to
Surviving the University

Bryan Nash

DE WARD
PUBLISHING COMPANY

Preface

I had no idea when I moved into my college dorm on a warm, starry night that my life would never be the same. Can I tell you a secret? I was a little scared. I was encompassed by new surroundings and new people. However, I was out of the nest and ready to spread my wings. Some days I limped along. Some days I soared. The next few years would consist of victory and defeat, success and failure, and many experiences worthy of reflection. I would make new friends, acquire new skills, and face new temptations.

Every day, Christians are engaged in warfare (Eph 6.11). College itself is a war comprised of many battles. Many students have pulled out of the driveway at home, a faithful Christian but allowed the spiritual man to be killed on the battlefield called the university. As a college student there are many battles you will fight. My hope is that this book will help you not only to survive, but to flourish.

I believe that every college student faces four battles. First, there is the battle of second thoughts. Quite a few students, after just a week months at the university, have concluded that there is no all-powerful Creator, there is no Savior, and there is no infallible, inspired writings. Many professors will be happy to challenge your faith. A person who responds intellectually is a rare breed. You must develop not only a heart faith but a head faith. In other words, know why you believe what you believe.

The second battlefield may not seem like a battlefield at all. It is the battle of seemingly small stuff. You know, the things that do not seem that important--like who your roommate is, whose drama you listen to, how many times you hit the snooze button, where you worship, and those little white lies. If Satan can convince you that these areas are not that important, he has you right where he wants you.

The third battle is the battle of sinful surroundings. Mom and Dad likely are not around to peer over your shoulder. You will have the opportunity to do things you did not even know existed. The Gentiles were inventors of evil things (Rom 1.30), but I am pretty sure college students could give them a run for their money. Will you accept or refuse these new offers?

The fourth battle is the battle of stewardship. If you feel like you never have enough time or money, there might be some helpful hints in these chapters from which you can benefit.

My goal in writing this book is to help you avoid the pitfalls that have ruined so many. These are the 12 essentials to success in the university setting. To succeed you must be purposeful, not complacent. Some of the suggestions in this book come from victory, while others come from my reflection on failure. The areas in which you are strong may be the areas in which I am weak. "But each one is tempted when he is lured and enticed by his own desire" (Jas 1.14). Nevertheless, after observation, reflection, and prayer, I have narrowed it down to a list of 12. Many of my dear friends lost their faith in college, and all of them had serious struggles in one or more of these areas. You will encounter many lackadaisical people, but if you understand these 12 survival tactics, you'll be a learner and a leader who loves the Lord.

Contents

Part Four: The Battle of Stewardship

Part One

The Battle of Second Thoughts

The Battle of Second Thoughts

As a Christian in college, your first battlefield is the classroom. Your faith will be challenged and perhaps even mocked. Satan works in the classroom as much as he does in the clubs. Many young people have quit the faith because they could not defend their faith intellectually with evidence.

Be ready to defend your beliefs. In 1 Peter 3.15, Christians are encouraged to be ready to defend their hope in Christ. The word *defense* is from the Greek word *apologia*, which means to answer or give a speech in defense of. It is also found in Acts 22.1; 25.16; 1 Corinthians 9.3; 2 Timothy 4.16; and Philippians 1.7, 17. The English word *apology* is derived from the Greek word *apologia*. The word *apology* means to confess oneself of a fault in search of forgiveness or a statement defending one's actions.[1] The latter is what Peter meant when he wrote, "…always being prepared to make a defense (*apologia*) to anyone who asks you for a reason for the hope that is in you…" (1 Pet 3.15). As Mark Twain once said, "Whatever you say, say it with conviction." In order to be a truly convicted Christian, you must know why you believe what you believe.

Many people are of the opinion that faith and logic cannot coexist. The Scriptures blatantly contradict this type of thinking. We read in Hebrews 11.1, "Now faith is the substance of things hoped for, the *evidence* of things not seen." In order to build a case and present a defense, you need evidence. We are fortunate to live in a time when there is an ample supply of scientific evidence pointing toward a Creator, His Son, and His Word. It's an ironic situation. As our technology improves and our understanding of the world deepens, the great minds of our day are realizing that maybe their minds are not so great after all.

Scientist, speaker, and author, Dr. Stephen C. Meyer said, "Scientists in the nineteenth century weren't aware of these things when they said naturalism accounts for everything. Thanks to the discoveries of the last five decades, we know a lot more today."[2] Many well-respected scientists are beginning to acknowledge the fact that there is a power greater than them.

Meyer also states, "Taken together, what we know today gives us heightened confidence from science that God exists. The weight of the evidence is very, very impressive. In fact, in my opinion it's sufficiently conclusive to say that theism provides the best explanation for the ensemble of scientific evidence."[3]

The next three chapters will introduce the evidence for God, His Word, and His Son. Don't run from this battle, and don't lose it.

Develop an Evidence-Based Belief in God

"Birds are closely related to lizards." I can still hear the voice of my ichthyology professor echoing through the upstairs room of one of the oldest buildings on campus. I stopped to collect my thoughts. "Did I hear her correctly?" I asked myself. The room reeked of formaldehyde, and this had a way of distracting me during my early morning class. I'm not much of a morning person, and the smell of preserved fish specimens never has helped me concentrate. Yes, I had heard correctly. And that wasn't the only challenging remark I would hear that semester.

Evolution is fact, and creation is false. That is the pre-dominant view among academics. The faith of many has been weakened as they sit through lecture after lecture describing our ancestry and the beginning of life. How did our society arrive at this point? Is evolutionary theory consistent and correct? Is there scientific evidence for the existence of God? This chapter is by no means a comprehensive study of the evolution- versus-creation debate, but it is a succinct, and hopefully, simple summary that will lay the groundwork for your understanding of the topic.

The Evolution of Evolution
In 1859, Charles Darwin published *The Origin of Species*. Darwin's writings were the product of his time spent on the

Galapagos Islands as well as the South American coast. *The Origin of Species* quickly became critically acclaimed in scientific circles. Darwin proposed the theory of macroevolution. In other words, all living things have a common ancestor. At this point, we must differentiate between macroevolution and microevolution. Microevolution, or the diversification within a given type,[4] has long been widely accepted, and it should be. You observe microevolution everyday. This is essentially what successful breeding is. My wife and I have a schnoodle, a cross between a schnauzer and a poodle. A good friend of mine owns a labradoodle, a cross between a labrador and a poodle (I give you these examples because anything ending in *oodle* is fun to say). Microevolution is common and inevitable. The idea of macroevolution, however, was brought to the masses by Darwin.

The advocates of macroevolution claim that fish were transformed into amphibians, amphibians into reptiles, reptiles into birds and mammals, with humans having the same ancestor as apes. In a nutshell, the proponents of Darwinism claim that if you trace your lineage back far enough, you will find a monkey climbing around in your family tree. If Darwin's conclusions are true, then there is no need for a Creator. Some textbooks go so far as to say that "Darwin gave biology a sound scientific basis by attributing the diversity of life to natural causes rather than supernatural creation."[5] Phillip Johnson, a critic of Darwinism and author of *Darwin on Trial*, states that "the whole point of Darwinism is to show that there is no need for a supernatural creator, because nature can do the creating by itself."[6] Francisco Ayala, a widely respected evolutionist, said that Darwin's greatest contribution was to show "living beings can be explained as a result of a natural process, natural selection, without any need to resort to a Creator or other external agent."[7] Author Nancy Pearcy made the issue cut and dried when she wrote, "You can have God or natural selection, but not both."[8]

While Charles Darwin was pondering the Galapagos Islands, Gregor Mendel was playing with pea plants. By experimenting with pea plants, Mendel discovered that traits are passed from parent to offspring. Furthermore, he discovered that traits are capable of skipping a generation. A trait can disappear within a generation only to reappear in the next. To put it in simpler terms, if your grandfather is bald, but your dad is not, you still have a chance of being a cue ball. On one hand, this information hurt the Darwinists because it showed that populations are stable. However, they focused on the fact that "an advantageous trait could survive and eventually become dominant in a population."[9] Mendel's findings were welcomed with open arms by early evolutionists.

The saying "A picture is worth a thousand words" is very true, but the pictures sketched by German biologist and friend of Charles Darwin, Ernst Haeckel, have spawned thousands upon thousands upon thousands of words. His controversial theory (published in 1866), as well as his drawings of embryos (published in 1874), have since been a source of confusion and criticism. Haeckel proposed that all organisms appear very similar in the earliest stages of development. The German biologist claimed that if you compare the embryo of a fish, a salamander, a tortoise, a chicken, a hog, a calf, and a rabbit with the embryonic stage of human development, you will find striking similarities. Were his findings correct? If so, does this mean we all have a common ancestor? Darwin thought so. He said, "Hardly any point gave me so much satisfaction when I was at work on the *Origin* as the explanation of the wide difference in many classes between the embryo and the adult animal, and the close resemblance of the embryos within the same class."[10]

At the root of evolutionary theory is this question: "Can living matter arise from nonliving matter?" Through the years several scientists have made it their mission to answer the question in the affirmative. In the 1920s, a Russian scientist named A.I. Oparin formulated a theory. He insisted that life arrived in stages. His explanation was that simple chemical compounds formed more complicated compounds. He claimed that this takes place due to energy in the environment. This energy, he speculated, is derived from things such as volcanoes, earthquakes, or light from the sun. These more complicated compounds formed even more complicated compounds and so on until eventually there was a living organism.

In 1953, Stanley Miller and Harold Urey conducted an experiment and, based on their findings, concluded that something similar to what A.I. Oparin explained could have taken place.[11] Miller and Urey attempted to imitate the atmosphere of primitive earth and then shoot sparks, simulating lightning, through the artificial atmosphere. After this was done, amino acids, the building blocks of life, were found.

Today, professors who believe in a Creator are in the minority. As Oxford evolutionist Richard Dawkins said, "The more you understand the significance of evolution, the more you are pushed away from an agnostic position towards atheism."[12] Tim Berra, author and Ohio State University professor, wrote, "Charles Darwin didn't want to murder God, as he once put it. But he did."[13]

Exposing the Evolutionary Evidence

Evolutionary biologist and historian of Cornell University, William Provine, made some strong statements regarding Darwinism. He said that if Darwinism explains the origin of mankind then five things must be true:

1. There's no evidence for God.
2. There's no life after death.
3. There's no absolute foundation for right and wrong.
4. There's no ultimate meaning for life.
5. People don't really have free will. [14]

What if you could show that Darwin's theory contains flaws? Then according to Provine, there is evidence for a God, the Intelligent Designer; there is life after death; there is an absolute foundation for right and wrong; life has an ultimate meaning; and people do have free will. In order to debunk Darwinism, we must look at the fossil record. According to Darwin, organisms will show very gradual change over time. Does the fossil record support this theory? The answer is, *no*.

According to Dr. Jonathan Wells, geologist and author of *Icons of Evolution: Why Much of What We Teach about Evolution is Wrong*, "Darwin knew the fossil record failed to support his tree. Darwin believed that future fossil discoveries would vindicate his theory, but that hasn't happened."[15] It is possible to trace generations of some species to a common ancestor. Let's use the example of dogs again since that is the animal with which many people are most familiar.

Imagine that you could trace a dog's family tree back many, many, many, many generations. Let's say, hypothetically, you were able to go all the way back and find that dog's 30th great-grandfather. Depending on the dog you use, you will likely find many different types of dogs in the family tree and maybe even a wolf. However, you would not find a turtle, a bird, an elephant or any other different type of animal. The fossil record confirms slight changes within a species, but no gradual changes through all organisms, as Darwin suggested. Wells declares, "Based on all this, I think it's reasonable for me, as a scientist, to say that maybe we should question our assumption that this common ancestor exists…it's a very, very shaky hypothesis. In fact, I would say it's disconfirmed. The evidence just doesn't support it."[16]

What are we to make of Haeckel's drawings that depict a fish, salamander, tortoise, chicken, hog, calf, rabbit, and human side-by-side? They appear to be very similar in the early stages of life. Does this mean we are all related? First, remember that these are drawings, not actual pictures. In the words of Wells, "…he doctored the drawings to make them look more similar than they really are. At any rate, his drawings misrepresent the embryo."[17] Second, it's not a fair representation of the animal kingdom. Haeckel essentially sought embryos that resembled each other. It's not a fair, unbiased sample. Furthermore, there are different stages of embryonic development, and Haeckel chose the stage in which most organisms resemble each other. Had he depicted an earlier stage or a later stage, all the embryos would appear drastically different. According to Wells, Haeckel chose the "midpoint" and did a very poor job of representing it.

Finally, we come to the Miller-Urey experiment which supposedly proved that living matter can arise from nothing. This experiment hinges on whether or not they correctly simulated the atmosphere of early earth. The general consensus is that these men did not do a good job of creating an atmosphere similar to planet earth. Even if they did, they only created amino acids, not living cells. In his critique on the Miller-Urey experiment, Wells points out that, "You would have to get the right number of the right kinds of amino acids to link up to create a protein molecule, and that would still be a long way from a living cell. Then you'd need dozens of protein molecules, again in the right sequence, to create a living cell. The odds against this are astonishing. The gap between nonliving chemicals and even the most primitive living organism is absolutely tremendous…It would be like a physicist doing an experiment to see if he can get a rock to fall upwards all the way to the moon."[18]

The fossil record does not support Darwin's claim of gradual change, Haeckel fudged drawings of embryos, and Miller and Urey did not accurately represent earth's atmosphere. Are you starting to see a trend? Let's examine a few more pieces of evidence and then you will be able to put together a compelling defense.

Lies about Limbs

Many animals share similar structures. For instance, wings, flippers, and the human hand have a comparable bone arrangement. This phenomenon is known as homology. Many point to these similarities as proof of macroevolution. But just because two things are similar, it does not mean that one emerged from the other. Imagine a newly developed subdivision in which all the houses look alike. Is it more logical to conclude that they were built by the same people who used similar materials, or that one house popped up and then several others followed? Clearly it is absurd to believe that there was not a designer. Although science does not have a definitive answer as to how and why structures are similar in different animals, the burden of proof lies on those who claim it is because of evolution. When scientists have difficulty explaining something they fall back on evolution. As one opponent of evolution stated, "What the textbook is saying is that similarity due to common ancestry is due to common ancestry…that's circular reasoning."[19]

Imperfect Parts

If you study evolutionist arguments, you are bound to stumble upon a branch of study referred to as dysteleology. Dysteleology is a branch of physiology that deals with supposed purposeless parts. For example, think about flightless birds. You will never see a penguin soaring through the sky. Why would God give them wings? Why do cave dwelling animals that spend their entire existence in the dark have eyes? There are numerous examples, but those will suffice. The argument is, if there is an Intelligent Designer, He would not create purposeless parts. Even more than that, His design should be flawless. If He creates something that is imperfect, how can we call Him intelligent? If you purchased a car and it had parts that did not work, you would say it was poorly and inefficiently designed.

For starters, physiologists are always learning more about the function of anatomical structures. For years it was thought that the appendix served no purpose. Thus, it would be an example of dysteleology. However, in recent times doctors have discovered that the appendix creates helpful bacteria that aid the digestive system. Furthermore, we now know that penguins use their wings as flippers.

When something is created there is always a trade-off. I learned this principle when playing sports video games as a kid. I always loved the games that allowed you to create a player. I created basketball players that were huge. My created player would be eight feet tall and 350 pounds. Although he was a great rebounder he failed miserably at everything else. Then I would create a player who was five feet tall and 120 pounds. He would be incredibly fast and a great ball handler, but he was too small to be a scoring threat. A designer cannot focus solely on one aspect, but must create something that functions as a whole. Consider the words of Dr. Stephen C. Meyer, regarding dysteleology:

> You could look at the screen and say, 'Bad design; it should have been bigger.' You could look at the keyboard and say, 'Bad design; should have been easier to use.' But the engineer isn't supposed to be creating the best screen, the best memory, and the best keyboard. He's supposed to be producing the best computer he can given certain size, weight, price, and portability requirements. Could the screen be bigger? Yes, but then portability suffers. Could the computer have more memory? Sure, but then the cost goes too high. So there are inevitable tradeoffs and compromises. Each individual part might be criticized for being suboptimal, but that's not the issue. The real issue is how well the overall laptop functions. That's how good engineering works, and that explains some of the examples of supposed dysteleology that are raised.[20]

Evidence for the Existence of God: All of a Sudden

The Big Bang Theory has been misunderstood. Some think that it is such a vile, evil concept that they will barely even utter the words. What may surprise you is that the basic principle helps the case for an Intelligent Designer. At the root of the theory is the idea that whatever happened was sudden and abrupt. Some scientists cannot fathom attributing the beginning to God, and therefore, outlandish theories have been proposed. However, progress has been made in academic circles due to the fact that virtually everyone agrees there was a brisk beginning. Dr. William Lane Craig states, "I would say that its *broad framework* is very securely established as a scientific fact."[21] Well-known physicist, Stephen Hawking wrote, "Almost everyone now believes that the universe, and time itself, had a beginning."[22] For years it was thought that the universe was "...a static, eternally existing object."[23] Today that idea is as laughable as the theory that the world is flat.

It is now accepted by virtually all, that life sprang into existence out of nothing all at once. The debate is over what, or Who, caused it to happen. Sometimes it is difficult to discern between information that is insightful and information that is impractical. However, you don't have to be a Ph.D. to realize that it is quite an intellectual stretch to believe that life emerged out of a soupy substance. Craig says:

> You see, the idea that things can come into being uncaused out of nothing, is worse than magic. At least when a magician pulls a rabbit out of a hat, there's the magician and the hat...We never see things coming into being uncaused out of nothing. Nobody worries that while he's away at work, say, a horse might pop into being, uncaused, out of nothing, in his living room, and be there defiling the carpet. We don't worry about those kinds of things, because they never happen.[24]

The fossil record also helps to establish the sudden nature of creation. The fact that the fossil record does not show gradual changes, but instead takes gigantic leaps is known as the Cambrian explosion or the Biological Big Bang. Although I do not believe every detail of what is called the Cambrian explosion (just as I do not believe every detail of the Big Bang Theory) at its core it shows that life emerged suddenly.

> When you look at the issue from the perspective of biological information, the best explanation is that intelligence was responsible for this otherwise inexplicable phenomenon. So when you encounter the Cambrian explosion with its huge and sudden appearance of radically new body plans, you realize you need lots of new biological information. Some of it would be encoded for in DNA although how that occurs is still an insurmountable problem for Darwinists. But on top of that, where does the new information come from that's not attributable to DNA? How does the hierarchal arrangement of cells, tissues, organs, and body plans develop? Darwinists don't have an answer. It's not even on their radar." [25]

Don't Change that Dial

Have you ever tried to tune to an AM radio station at night on an old radio? The station comes and goes, but if you fine tune the knob and the wind blows the clouds in just the right direction, you can pick it up. It appears to scientists that the earth's forces and conditions have been fine tuned. From gravity to gases, everything is fine tuned perfectly for humans to live. It has been said that there are more than thirty parameters that require precise tuning to support life. If one of these were changed the most miniscule amount, life would cease. For example, a small adjustment in gravitational force, just one part in ten thousand billion, billion, billion, would result in humans and animals being crushed.

There is an ample supply of evidence for Creation. Our job as Christians is to educate ourselves so that we can intelligently defend our belief and our Creator. When you look in the mirror remember you are "fearfully and wonderfully made" (Psa 139.14), and when you observe the setting sun, the vast valleys, and the raging rivers, remember, He has "made them all" (Psa 104.24).

Questions for personal reflection or group study

1. Why do you think so many people put their faith in evolution instead of creation?

2. What experiences have you had so far with evolutionary teaching? What was your reaction?

3. Why is Darwinism not a good explanation of the origin of life? Haeckel's embryos? The Miller-Urey experiment?

4. Explain and refute the argument of imperfect parts (dysteleology).

5. What do you find to be the most compelling evidence for creation? Why?

6. Find someone who believes in creation and someone who believes in evolution. Ask each why they believe the way they do. Write down what they tell you and discuss your findings with others. You may be surprised by the answers you receive.

7. Write a short defense of creation. (It might be a good idea to keep this in your wallet or purse so you can refer to it often.)

Develop an Evidence-Based Belief in God's Word

"The first book we will read is the book of the Job," said my English literature professor enthusiastically, as he handed out the syllabus for the upcoming semester. We would be reading Job alongside the classic works of Shakespeare and Homer. In the eyes of the wiry, passionate professor, the book of Job was just another piece of literature to be read and discussed as fiction. I wrote an essay on the book of Job as I did for plays and poetry. In college classrooms all over the world, the Bible is viewed as just another book of myths, imaginary people, and fantasy worlds. However, upon careful consideration one will find that the Bible is a book unlike any other. In this chapter, we will answer three questions: First, how did we get the Bible? Second, has it been preserved and translated correctly? Third, what about the alleged contradictions and discrepancies in the Bible?

How did we get the Bible?
Materials and Methods
Through the course of my relatively short life I have written on several materials and used several writing instruments. I have attempted to color inside the lines with crayons, I have heard the unpleasant screech of chalk on a blackboard, and I have erased mistakes from paper with the help of a pencil

eraser. Those who lived through biblical times used different materials as well.

Stone served as the first piece of paper in almost every civilization. The Ten Commandments were written on stone (Ex 31.18), as was the law after the Israelites had crossed the Jordan (Josh 8.32). Clay was common in the countries of Assyria and Babylonia. Archaeologists have found vast libraries of clay tablets in these regions. Ezekiel was told to write on clay in Ezekiel 4.1.

Arguably, the most important writing material of the ancient world was papyrus. Papyrus was a reed that grew in the shallow lakes and rivers of Egypt and Syria. *The Cambridge History of the Bible* recounts how papyrus was prepared. "The reeds were stripped and cut lengthwise into thin narrow slices before being beaten and pressed together into two layers set at right angles to each other. When dried the whitish surface was polished smooth with a stone or other implement."[1] Sheets of papyrus were glued together and wound around a stick to form a scroll. These were the first "books."

Vellum and parchment are two terms used interchangeably to refer to animal skins that were prepared for the sole purpose of writing. Vellum manuscripts (copies of the New Testament in Greek) are some of the most beautiful and ornate. Some have been found that were dyed purple and inscribed with gold letters. Vellum was used because of its durability. Papyrus was fragile and in limited supply, so from the fourth century on, vellum was the primary writing material used.

Today, those writing with pen and paper will either write in cursive or print. Similarly, there are two writing styles found on ancient manuscripts: uncials and cursives. Professor Neil Lightfoot describes uncial manuscripts as those written, "…in large letters without intervening spaces between the words and with no marks of punctuation."[2] Today's equivalent would be writing everything in uppercase with no punctuation and no spaces between words. While this practice may seem odd and difficult today, it was second nature to those who lived long ago. The other type of writing is referred to as miniscule or cursive writing and is similar to modern cursive in that it was a script of smaller letters in running hand.[3]

The style of writing on a manuscript is used to determine its date. How large are the letters? How much space is there between the letters? How many columns are there? These are just a few of the questions investigated when dating manuscripts.

The Canon

The Bible is comprised of 66 books. There are 39 books in the Old Testament, and 27 books in the New Testament. Through the ages, there have been many religious writings. In the first and second centuries there were other letters written to churches by various individuals. Why do these 66 books make up the Bible? The answer to this question is found by studying what is referred to as the canon of the Scriptures. The English word *canon* is derived from the Greek word *kanon* and the Hebrew word *qaneh*. Its basic meaning is *reed*, which is where we get our English word *cane*. Since a reed was sometimes used as a measuring rod, the word *kanon* came to mean a standard or rule. Therefore, if one speaks of the canon or canonical writings, he is speaking of those books which are regarded as inspired by God and should be considered Scripture.

It is crucial to understand that men did not decide which books were inspired. In the words of Norman Geisler, "A book is not the Word of God because it is accepted by the people of God. Rather, it was accepted by the people of God because it is the Word of God. That is, God gives the book its divine authority, not the people of God. They merely recognize the divine authority God gives to it."[4] In the words of Lightfoot, "The church does not control the canon, the canon controls the church."[5]

Geisler also writes, "The initial reason for collecting and preserving the inspired books was that they were prophetic. That is, since they were written by an apostle or prophet of God, they must be valuable, and if valuable, they should be preserved. This reasoning is apparent in apostolic times, by the collection and circulation of Paul's epistles."[6] Books were rejected if they contained historical or geographical inaccuracy, or if they taught doctrines that contradicted already-accepted Scripture.

It seems that in the time of Christ, the canon of the Old Testament had already been established. Jesus and others constantly referred to Scripture that was universally accepted as inspired (John 7.42; 13.18; 17.12; 19.24, 28, 36–37; Acts 8.32; Rom 1.2; 4.3; 9.17; 10.11; 11.2; 16.26; 1 Cor 15.3–4; Gal 3.8; 1 Tim 5.18; 2 Pet 1.20–21). Also, the Hebrew Scriptures were separated into three parts and Jesus acknowledged this division in Luke 24.44.

It did not take long for the for the New Testament canon to begin coming together. Justin Martyr wrote early in the second century that the church read the "...memoirs of the apostles or the writings of the prophets."[7] Late in the second century substantial lists of the New Testament books appear and by AD 367 Athanasius recorded a list of all the accepted New Testament books:

> Again it is not tedious to speak of the books of the New Testament. These are, the four gospels, according to Matthew, Mark, Luke and John. Afterwards, the Acts of the Apostles and Epistles (called Catholic), seven, viz. of James, one; of Peter, two; of John, three; after these, one of Jude. In addition, there are fourteen Epistles of Paul written in this order. The first, to the Romans; then two to the Corinthians; after these, to the Galatians; next, to the Ephesians; then to the Philippians; then to the Colossians; after

these, two to the Thessalonians, and that to the Hebrews; and again, two to Timothy; one to Titus; and lastly, that to Philemon. And besides, the Revelation of John.[8]

The Old Testament is recorded in Hebrew, while the New Testament is in Greek. So how do we have an English Bible today? To find the answer we must go all the way back to the fourteenth century. John Wycliffe sought to reform the Catholic church, and one of his goals was to translate the Scriptures, which were, at that time in Latin, into English. This was completed in 1382. Then in 1388, John Purvey, a friend of Wycliffe, revised Wycliffe's version. Purvey's corrected version lasted until the sixteenth century.

The efforts of William Tyndale, however, are most important in our search for understanding how the English Bible came to be. Tyndale sought not to translate the Scriptures from Latin as Wycliffe did, but rather to translate from the original Hebrew and Greek. Tyndale was met with opposition, but in 1526 the first English copies of the New Testament were brought into England. Tyndale was berated and eventually burned at the stake in 1536. Bibles were burned, but nothing could stop the movement that had begun.

Following Tyndale's work, several versions were made available and many crucial events transpired. The next event of monumental significance was in 1611. In 1604, King James held a meeting to discuss religious tolerance. In the midst of the meeting, Dr. John Reynolds suggested a new translation of the Bible. King James was adamant that this translation not be representative of the translator's opinions, but instead, stay true to the original text. In 1607, 48 Hebrew or Greek scholars were selected to begin work on this translation. The work was completed in 1611 and on the title page were the words, "Appointed to be read in the Churches." The King James Version is still widely used today. Since 1611, many new versions which hold true to the original text have become available. Thanks to the sacrifices and scholarship of men like Wycliffe and Tyndale, we can hold in our hands the inspired word of God in English. [9]

Has it Been Preserved Correctly?
It Passes the Tests

Ok, so the Bible is available in English. How do we know it has been translated correctly? Is it possible that we could read the same message as people did thousands of years ago? The impression that the Bible has been mistranslated is a major hang-up for many people. Perhaps they believe in a God, but they don't see how it is possible, or even rational, to believe that we could have His original words in our hands today.

In answering these questions it is only fair to apply the same tests to the Bible that we apply to ancient, secular writings. These tests are not used to determine whether a book is inspired but rather to determine whether or not it reads closely to the original. For example, no one argues that Homer's *Iliad* should not be read in literature class because it has been mistranslated. Anyone who would say such a thing would be laughed at because the *Iliad* has passed all the tests of historical reliability. So, how does the Bible stack up?

The first test applied to works of antiquity, or ancient writings, is the bibliographical test. The bibliographical test asks this question: How accurate are the copies we have considering the number of manuscripts and the time interval between the original and the earliest copies? The short answer is that the Bible passes this test with flying colors. As of 1999, there were about 25,000 manuscript copies or pieces of manuscripts of the New Testament. No other document even comes close. Homer's *Iliad* comes in second place with 643 ancient manuscripts. [10] As one expert said, "…to be skeptical of the resultant text of the New Testament books is to allow all of classical antiquity to slip into obscurity, for no documents of the ancient period are as well attested bibliographically as the New Testament."[11] Frederick G. Kenyon, librarian of the British Museum adds this,

> Besides number, the manuscripts of the New Testament differ from those of classical authors. In no other case is the interval between the composition of the book and the date of the earliest extant manuscripts so short as in that of the New Testament. The latter part of the first century; the earliest extant manuscripts are of the fourth century-say from 250–300 years. This may sound like a considerable interval, but it is nothing to that which parts most of the great classical authors from their earliest manuscripts. We believe that we have in all essentials an accurate text of the seven extant plays of Sophocles; yet the earliest substantial manuscript upon which it is based was written more than 1,400 years after the poet's death.[12]

The second test is the external evidence test. This test asks the question, "Do other historic materials confirm or deny the document?" The Bible passes this test as well. We will delve deeper into this idea in the next chapter, but for now it will suffice to say that historic writings confirm the biblical accounts. Suetonius, who lived early in the second century, affirms some of the events Luke recorded in the book of Acts.[13] Suetonius wrote of these events about 75 years after they took place, making him a credible source. This would be like people in their 70s telling you about events that took place in the 1940s. They were likely not an eyewitness, but they were close enough to the events to talk about them intelligently. Well known historian, Josephus (AD 37–100), verifies many of the events in the Bible as well.

People, Places, and Things

If the biblical text has not been preserved, you would expect to find errors when it refers to people, places, or things. This is not the case. Archaeologist Nelson Glueck states, "Scores of archaeological findings have been made which confirm in clear outline or exact detail historical statements of the Bible."[14] Volumes of books have been written cataloging archaeological finds and the accuracy of the Scriptures.

What About the Contradictions and Discrepancies?

This question posed by skeptics usually stands alone, but it could well be asked alongside our second question, "Has it been preserved correctly?" because it is a question asked by historians to determine if a document is credible and mirrors the original. If it contains contradictions, then clearly something has been lost in the copying process.

Some have claimed that the Bible contains 200,000 errors. How are we to answer such a claim? First, we must understand how that figure was attained. These figures are counts of scribal errors. Let's say that a scribe misspelled a word and there are 5,000 copies of that manuscript. Well, someone now says that the Bible contains 5,000 errors. See how misleading these numbers are? Furthermore, almost all textual variations are insignificant. They center on words like "and" or "the." In some cases word order may be the culprit. Perhaps an early version read, "the Lord Jesus Christ" then it is determined that "Jesus Christ the Lord" is a more accurate rendering. Such trivial things should in no way make us question the inspiration of Scripture. [15]

Oftentimes, alleged discrepancies stem from our lack of understanding. As Josh McDowell says, "Fallible interpretations do not mean fallible revelation."[16] Rational, reasonable thinking will answer most questions. For example, Judas' death is often cited as a contradiction. In Matthew 27.5, Judas "…went and hanged himself." In Acts 1.18, Judas fell and "…burst open in the middle and all his bowels gushed out." Likely, Judas hanged himself and then the limb broke or the rope grew weak resulting in his falling upon the jagged edges of rocks. A trip to the supposed site of Judas' death reveals the perfect location for this to take place.

This chapter would be incomplete if the power and providence of God were not emphasized. In Mark 13.31, Jesus said, "Heaven and earth will pass away, but my words will by no means pass away." If God can create and sustain the earth and all that is in it, do you not think he can preserve His words for all generations to read and understand? The Bible is not just another book. It is the inspired word of God.

Questions for personal reflection or group study

1. On what materials did people write in biblical times? Describe the two writing styles.

2. What is meant by the word *canon*?

3. In what language was the Old Testament originally recorded? The New Testament?

4. Draw a timeline and label the main events in the making of the English Bible.

5. Are you confident the Bible has been preserved correctly? If so, list some reasons why.

6. How would you respond to someone who says the Bible is full of errors and contradictions?

7. Hopefully you've written your defense of creation. Now, write a short defense of God's word.

Develop an Evidence-Based Belief in God's Son

I always enjoyed philosophy class, maybe because there are no wrong answers. My professor always seemed less than confident. I imagine it is hard to be confident in your material when you believe there is no absolute truth. We studied the proposals of Plato, the ideas of Aristotle, and occasionally the judgment of a man named Jesus. Jesus was put into the category of great teacher.

In this chapter we will examine the evidence for Jesus Christ. First, we will look at external evidence (What do historical sources outside of the Bible tell us about Him?). Second, we will look at the internal evidence. (What does the Bible record about Christ? Was Jesus a mere man or the Messiah?)

External Evidence

Although some do try to deny that Jesus ever lived, no serious scholar would make such a statement. Historical writings about the life of Jesus are abundant. Tacitus, a Roman historian, wrote,

> Hence to suppress the rumor, he (Nero) falsely charged with guilt, and punished the most exquisite tortures, the persons commonly called Christians, who were hated for their enormities. Christus, the founder of the name,

was put to death by Pontius Pilate, procurator of Judea
in the reign of Tiberius: but the pernicious superstition,
repressed a time, broke out again, not only through Judea,
where the mischief originated, but through the city of
Rome also."[1]

Lucian, a second-century Greek, said, "The Christians,
you know, worship a man to this day—the distinguished
personage who introduced their novel rites, and was crucified on that account."[2] Lucian never argued that Christ was
not a real person. He accepted that fact.

Suetonius, another Roman historian, wrote, "As the Jews
were making constant disturbances at the instigation of
Chrestus (another misspelling), he (Claudius) expelled them
from Rome."[3]

Pliny, governor of Bithynia recorded these words about
Christians, "They were in the habit of meeting on a certain
fixed day before it was light, when they sang in alternate
verse a hymn to Christ as to a god…"[4]

Mara Bar-Serapion, a first century philosopher wrote
about Christ alongside of Socrates, Plato, and Pythagoras.
Mara Bar-Serapion was not a believer, but his writings do
establish that Christ was regarded as a historical figure.

Historian Josephus wrote in his *Jewish Antiquities*, "Now
there was about this time Jesus, a wise man, for he was a
doer of wonderful works, a teacher of such men as receive
the truth with pleasure. He drew over to him both many of
the Jews and many of the Gentiles. When Pilate, at the sug-
gestion of the principal men among us, had condemned him
to the cross, those that loved him at the first did not forsake
him."[5] Josephus also wrote, "a council of judges…brought
before it the brother of Jesus, the so-called Christ…"[6]

Denying that Jesus ever lived is an ignorant stance to
take. We do not doubt that men such as Thomas Edison or
George Washington lived. We know they lived because we
can read about them in the annals of history. Similarly, Jesus

is a historical figure. As one scholar said, "It is not possible to explain the rise of the Christian church or the writing of the Gospels and the stream of tradition that lies behind them without accepting the fact that the Founder of Christianity actually existed."[7]

Internal Evidence
The Claims of Christ

We have established that Jesus did live on this earth. Jesus posed an intriguing question in Mark 8.27: "Who do people say that I am?" In answering this question we must take into account who Jesus said He was. Jesus said He was the Son of God on many occasions. In Mark 14.61, the high priest asked, "'Are you the Christ, the Son of the Blessed?' And Jesus said, 'I am…'"

Not only did Jesus claim to be the Messiah, He claimed to be like God the Father. In answering the Jews, Jesus said in John 10.30, "I and the Father are one." One of the reasons the Jews sought to kill Christ was because they understood His claims of equality. "This was why the Jews were seeking all the more to kill him, because not only was he breaking the Sabbath, but he was even calling God his own Father, making himself equal with God" (John 5.18). In response to this Jesus said,

> Truly, truly, I say to you, the Son can do nothing of his own accord, but only what he sees the Father doing. For whatever the Father does, that the Son does likewise. For the Father loves the Son and shows him all that he himself is doing. And greater works than these will he show him, so that you may marvel. For as the Father raises the dead and gives them life, so also the Son gives life to whom he will. The Father judges no one, but has given all judgment to the Son, that all may honor the Son, just as they honor the Father. Whoever does not honor the Son does not honor the Father who sent him. (John 5.19–23)

Jesus answered the scribes and Pharisees in John 8.19 by saying, "You know neither me nor my Father. If you knew me, you would know my Father also" (John 8.19). In John 14.1, Christ said that anyone who believed in God should also believe in Him.

Jesus claimed to be the Messiah and God, and He taught with authority. Throughout the Sermon on the Mount Jesus used the phrase, "I say to you" to contrast the popular thinking and teaching of his day (Matt 5.20, 22, 26, 28, 32, 34, 44). When he finished speaking "the crowds were astonished at His teaching for he was teaching them as one who had authority, and not as their scribes" (Matt 7.28–29).

Furthermore, Jesus accepted praise during His ministry. In Acts 10.25–26, Cornelius fell down and worshipped Peter, but Peter told him to get up. Peter said, "I too am a man" (Acts 10.26). Never did Jesus say, "I too am a man." Jesus accepted praise and worship. In John 9.35–39, Jesus healed a blind man and the man worshipped Him. Matthew records that those who saw Jesus walk on water worshipped Him (Matt 14.33). Jesus never condemned His followers for praising Him. If He made no claim to be the Messiah He would have said as Peter did, "Stand up. I too am a man." Jesus never uttered those words. As one person said, "A man who can read the New Testament and not see that Christ claims to be more than a man, can look over the sky at high noon on a cloudless day and not see the sun."

Jesus was a historical figure. He claimed to be the Savior, and we can trust those words to be His because they have been preserved correctly. So, we now must come to a conclusion. Was Jesus crazy or the Christ? If He were lying, and He knew He was lying, then Jesus was either stupid or a psychopath. He would be a fool to die for something He knew was a lie, and only a crazy man would claim to be God, if in fact He weren't.

Is it logical to conclude that Jesus was a chronic liar? Church historian Philip Schaff doesn't think so:

The hypothesis of imposture is so revolting to moral as well as common sense, that its mere statement is its condemnation. No scholar of any decency and self-respect would now dare to profess it openly. How, in the name of logic, common sense, and experience, could an impostor---that is a deceitful, selfish, depraved man---have invented, and consistently maintained from the beginning to end, the purest and noblest character known in history with the most perfect air of truth and reality? How could he have conceived and successfully carried out a plan of unparalleled beneficence, more magnitude, and sublimity, and sacrificed his own life for it, in the face of the strongest prejudices of his people and ages?[8]

If Jesus wasn't a chronic liar, is it possible that He could have been an insane man who really believed He was God's Son? Philosopher Peter Kreeft writes this about insanity:

A measure of your insanity is the size of the gap between what you think you are and what you really are. If I think I am the greatest philosopher in America, I am only an arrogant fool; if I think I am Napolean, I am probably over the edge; if I think I am a butterfly, I am fully embarked from the sunny shores of sanity. But if I think I am God, I am even more insane because the gap between anything finite and the infinite God is even greater than the gap between two finite things, even a man and butterfly.[9]

After examining the insight and intellect that comprised Christ's communication, psychiatrist J.T. Fisher makes this observation:

If you were to take the sum total of all authoritative articles ever written by the most qualified of psychologists and psychiatrists on the subject of mental hygiene—if you were to combine them and refine them and cleave out the excess verbiage—if you were to take the whole of the meat and none of the parsley, and if you were to have these unadulterated bits of pure scientific knowledge concisely ex-

pressed by the most capable of living poets you wouldhave
an awkward and incomplete Sermon on the Mount. And it
would suffer immeasurably through comparison. For nearly
two thousand years the Christian world has been holding
in its hands the answer to its restless and fruitless yearn-
ings. Here rests the blueprint for successful human life with
optimism, mental health, and contentment.[10]

To say that Jesus was a lunatic is even more preposterous
than accusing Him of deceit. Jesus was not a fibber, and He
was not a fool. So, who was He? There's only one answer
left. He's the foundation of our faith, the Son of God who
brought forgiveness (John 1.29). A popular apologist, Josh
McDowell, wrote:

> Who you decide Jesus Christ is must not be an idle intel-
> lectual exercise. You cannot put Him on the shelf of great
> moral teacher. That is not a valid option. He is either a liar,
> a lunatic, or the Lord. You must make a choice. 'But,' as
> the apostle John wrote, 'these have been written that you
> may believe that Jesus is the Christ, the Son of God'; and
> more important, 'that believing you may have life in His
> name' (John 20.31). The evidence is clearly in favor of Jesus
> as Lord. However, some people reject the clear evidence
> because of moral implications involved. There needs to be a
> moral honesty in the above consideration of Jesus as either
> liar, lunatic, or Lord and God.[11]

If you're still not convinced, consider one more pieces of
internal evidence.

The Resurrection

Christianity is a unique religion in that it is the only belief
system that claims an empty tomb of its founder. Not only
did Jesus fulfill many prophecies written years before, but He
also claimed that He would be raised from the dead (Matt
12.40; 16.21; 17.9, 22–23; 20.18–19; 27.63). Everything rises

and falls on the resurrection. Without it, the early disciples would have had no hope because Christ would not be who He claimed He was.

William Lane Craig wrote,

> Without the belief in the resurrection the Christian faith could not have come into being. The disciples would have remained crushed and defeated men. Even had they continued remembering Jesus as their beloved teacher, his crucifixion would have forever silenced any hopes of his being the Messiah. The cross would have remained the sad and shameful end of his career. The origin of Christianity therefore hinges on the belief of the early disciples that God had raised Jesus from the dead.[13]

We have already studied the fact that Jesus was a historical figure. That can not be argued. There are two other facts about Him with which virtually all historians agree. First, He was crucified. Second, His tomb was empty. His tomb was empty! Because this has been accepted as fact by all rational people, we must now ask the central question: How did a dead body disappear? Through the years several theories have been offered. Let's look at each one and see if it holds any weight.

First, the swoon theory. This theory states that Jesus did not really die on the cross, but that He fainted, and after several hours in the cool air of a tomb, He revived. We must realize that Roman soldiers were extremely skilled in what they did. Mistakes were not allowed. When they came to the body of Jesus on the cross they did not break His legs because they knew He was already dead (John 19.31–33). One of the soldiers, however, pierced His side with a spear (John 19.34) leaving no doubt. Let's say for a moment that Jesus did just swoon. How could a bloodied, beaten man who had survived a crucifixion have the strength to roll away the stone in front of the tomb? Today, few, if any, hold this position because it is so ridiculous.

Second, the stolen body theory. This theory claims that the disciples came and stole the body during the night. This theory seems to have begun shortly after the resurrection (Matt 28.12–13). How did the disciples get past the guards? Perhaps the guards had fallen asleep. If that were the case, how could the disciples have rolled back the stone without waking the guards? What about the clothes in the tomb (John 20.3–7)? As Merril Tenney said, "No robbers would ever have rewound the wrappings in their original shape, for there would not have been time to do so. They would have flung the cloths down in disorder and fled with the body. Fear of detection would have made them act as hastily as possible."[14] If the disciples had stolen the body, they would know the resurrection was a hoax. The disciples carried this belief all the way to painful deaths. Would you die for something if you knew it was a lie?

Third, the hallucination theory. This theory states that people who saw the risen Christ hallucinated. This would mean that many people had the exact same hallucination. Therefore, "Mary Magdalene and the other Mary" (Matt 28.1, 9), Peter (Luke 24.34), two people traveling to Emmaus (Luke 24.13–31), the apostles without Thomas (John 20.19–23), the apostles with Thomas (John 20.26–29), the disciples by the Sea of Tiberias (John 21.1), five hundred others (1 Cor 15.6), and James (1 Cor 15.7), all had the same hallucination. There is no way this could have happened.

Fourth, the mistaken identity theory. This theory is based on the idea that those who claimed to see Jesus just mistook Him for someone else. What are the odds? We have just noted how many people saw Jesus. Could all those people have been confused?

Fifth, the myth theory. This theory states that the resurrection developed over time as do many tall tales. For this to be the case, many years would have needed to pass. Talk of the resurrection, as well as writing, started immediately.

Enough time simply would not have elapsed for an exaggerated story to be passed down through the generations.

Sixth, the wrong tomb theory. The people who buy in to this theory believe that those who witnessed an empty tomb ignorantly stumbled upon the wrong tomb. The women knew exactly where the tomb was (Mark 15.47). Peter and John later went to the same tomb (John 20.2–8). Were they lost also? Finally, an angel was at the tomb (Matt 28.6). Did the angel lose his bearings? This theory is no better than the rest.

If people wanted to stop belief in the resurrection for good, all they would have had to do was go to the tomb and pull out the dead body of Jesus. They would have gone to the tomb, retrieved the body, held it for all to see and said, "Look. Here is the body. Now quit saying He has raised from the dead." Do you know why no one did that? There was not a body in the tomb. A person has to make a decision. Either you believe silly theories that do not stand up to scrutiny, or you believe that Jesus is the risen Son of God. Which makes more sense?

Questions for Personal Reflection or Group Study

1. How would you respond to someone who tells you that Jesus is a fictional character?

2. Who did Jesus claim to be? Why is this important in establishing Jesus as the Christ?

3. Do you think Jesus was a liar? Why or why not?

4. Do you think Jesus was a crazed madman? Why or why not?

5. Do you think Jesus was the Messiah, the Son of God? Why or why not?

6. Why should the prophecies of Jesus increase our faith in Him?

7. List the six theories pertaining to the resurrection and discuss why they should be rejected.

Part Two

The Battle of Seemingly Small Stuff

The Battle of Seemingly Small Stuff

Richard Carlson has written a best selling series *Don't Sweat the Small Stuff.* While many of us would do well to live a more relaxed life, the truth of the matter is that Satan wants us to view many things as "small stuff." We can easily fall into the trap of thinking that murder, drug addiction, stealing, etc. are "big things" and everything else is "small stuff." As long as we are at church on Sunday morning and do not have our picture on the wall at the post office we are ok, right? Wrong. The way we conduct ourselves during what may seem like menial tasks is important. In this section, we will look at some areas that are often filed away under "small stuff" and discuss why they are crucial to the Christian.

These are the battles that many people think are not important. They leave their shield and sword behind because they do not even see it as a battle. I have known people who have lost their faith because they failed to fight these five battles.

Maintain a Good Relationship with Your Roommate

When I walked into my dorm I was greeted by a tall, awkward man in a Hawaiian shirt. The first few buttons were undone revealing a tuft of chest hair. "Hi," he squeaked, "I'm Bo." (Names have been changed to protect the not-so-innocent.) Bo was about twelve years older than I and just starting junior college. You are never too old to get an education, but his reasons were amusing. "So what have you done since you graduated high school?" I inquired. "Well, mostly just hang out at the mall." "Great," I thought to myself, "I've got a real winner for a roommate." Bo quit after a couple of weeks. However, he did come back the following year. This stint was short-lived. Maybe it was because security tacked up wanted posters of him all over campus.

My next roommate was a guy I already knew. We will call him Matt. Unbeknownst to me, Matt had arranged to be my roommate during the summer. Apparently he was unaware of the fact that I thought he was one of the most obnoxious people I had ever met. However, after living with him for a few months my feelings changed. Now, he was *the most obnoxious person I had ever met.* He was the type of person who bragged about how hard he could punch and displayed empty Vodka bottles for decoration. After someone in the dorm threatened his life, Matt had the epiphany that it would be more economical for him to live somewhere else.

Third… third was… honestly, I have forgotten his name. You can probably guess that we did not talk much. He spent a lot of time at his parents' house and I rarely saw him. All that I remember is that he never slept, and he ate a lot, but I suppose that describes quite a few college students.

I finally got fortunate with number four, Daniel. Daniel was my doubles partner on the tennis team and ended up being a very dear friend. Although it has been a while since we have talked, I still consider him one my best buds.

The first two years of college I had a roommate, while the last two years I lived on my own. I can honestly say the worst times were with the bad roommates, the best times were with the good roommate, and living alone was somewhere in between.

College is all about learning, and one of the things you have to learn how to do is get along with different types of people. Granted, it is a lifelong endeavor, but when you are suddenly placed in a confined area with someone you have never met, you either learn quickly or learn to be miserable.

With whom should you room? It is amazing how little thought some people give to this. They do extensive research to determine which college they should attend, devote countless hours to picking a major, tediously make their schedule, but then live with whoever they hear needs a roommate. You may be in a situation like I was in and have no choice. However, if you are privileged to be able to choose someone, why not choose someone who will help you avoid temptation? It is true that just because you find a roommate at church, this is no guarantee this person will encourage you spiritually, and sometimes those who live with people who are not Christians, end up doing just fine. I would venture to say those are the exceptions, not the rule. We read in 1 Corinthians 15.33, "Do not be deceived: 'Bad company ruins good morals.'" The morals of many have been ruined during the college years, and if you trace it back, it all started with choosing who you should live with. Let's consider a process for finding a good roommate, the type of person you will want to choose, and some potential problems you may encounter.

The Process

1. Get involved early. Find the church you want to be a part of before your first semester ever starts. Take a weekend to visit and get acquainted with the people there. You may meet someone else doing the same thing, or you may meet someone there currently who needs a roommate for the upcoming semester. College students are very transient. If neither one of these things happens, find someone you hit it off with and ask them to give you a call if they hear of anything. Also, many churches, especially in college towns, have an email list or facebook page you can be a part of and get in the loop before you ever move. Chances are, if you are proactive you will be able to find a good roommate long before classes ever begin.

2. Ask around at other churches in your area. While this may not work very well if you are attending a college across the country, if you are going to a school fairly close to home, there is a good possibility someone from another congregation in your area will be attending the same school. Visit or call the churches within a reasonable distance and find out if they have someone in the same predicament as you. They will be more than happy to help.

3. Wait. A third option is to simply wait. If possible, live by yourself the first semester and then once you have gotten your feet wet, try to find someone. This approach has many advantages. First, it is one less adjustment you will have to make. Moving, starting classes, and adjusting to your new schedule can be stressful enough, but having to do all of this while also becoming acquainted with your new roommate can be too much for some people. Second, you'll be able to really get to know someone before you choose to live together. After being in town for a semester, hopefully you'll know quite a few people and you can make a wise choice. Third, you will have more time to find a place to live. Not only will you become more acquainted with whom you want to live, you will learn *where* you want to live. Some people sign a lease on the first room they look at and regret it later. The drawback to waiting is that you may find yourself alone for the whole year. Many people are required, due to written or verbal agreement, to stay where they are for two semesters. However, if waiting awhile before finding a roommate is a viable option for you, it may be your best choice.

The Person

What type of person should you live with? As already mentioned, it would be wise to live with a Christian. Hopefully, a Christian roommate will help you do three things:

1. Avoid temptations. Satan is a roaring lion (1 Pet 5.8), and he loves to prey on college students. There is definitely strength in numbers on the battlefield, and living with someone who wants the same thing out of life as you do, is an immeasurable benefit.

2. Attend services. College students are notorious for sleeping in, especially on the weekends. Living with someone who will hold you accountable and help you get up and get moving on Sunday is a huge plus.

3. Be active in your local church. Apartments and dorms where multiple Christians live always seem to be the gathering spot. It is easy to organize a Bible study or just a time to hang out when there are already a few members of the church living together in a given area. Also, chances are that if you have multiple roommates, you will be living somewhere large enough to have plenty of people over. This was one major drawback to living alone. I had a tiny, little apartment and there was no way I could have anybody over to my place. Not only will you be more likely to spend time with other Christians if you live with a Christian, it will also be much easier to stay informed and "in the loop" if you live with another member of the church.

Living with a Christian is no doubt important, but there are a couple of other things you might want to consider. For starters, what type of schedule does the person keep? Is he a night owl or an early bird? I can still vividly remember Matt yelling obscenities at the TV at 3:00 a.m. on multiple occasions. Needless to say, that's neither when, nor how I like to be awakened. Also, you might want to find out how dirty, or shall we say hygienically-challenged, your potential roommate is. The number one complaint I have heard of college students and their roommates is this: "He is so dirty!" Number two is this: "She is such a clean freak!" Those are just a couple of things to keep to mind.

Handling Problems

When you live with someone who has a different temperament, a different upbringing, and different interests, conflict will likely occur. Just ask any married couple. Seeing someone occasionally on the weekends is one thing, living with their quirks is something entirely different. Trust me. I'm quite quirky.

First, learn to appreciate differences in people. I highly recommend Florence Littauer's book, *Personality Plus*.[1] She identifies four different personality types as well as their strengths and weaknesses. This book is a must read for those who want to better understand themselves and others.

The first personality is powerful. Mr. Powerful comes out of the womb and immediately wants to be in charge. He wants life his way. Mr. Powerful is very goal-oriented and has the potential to become a great leader, but he tends to make enemies along the path to success. He has high energy, but he can be hurtful. He makes a magnificent manager, but he has difficulty knowing how to be a boss without being bossy. If you find yourself living with a powerful person, clearly divide areas of responsibility. The powerful personality feels like he has been put on this earth to lead the dummies through life. If you are by nature a passive person, your powerful roommate might try to turn you into his own personal slave. Make sure chores are divided, and each person knows his responsibilities.

Next, we will consider the opposite of Mr. Powerful, the peaceful personality. Mr. Peaceful is the type of person who loves to relax and will avoid conflict or offending at all costs. Although he is quiet and low-key, he makes friends easily and appears to be everyone's favorite person because of his kind, unassuming nature. Although the Mr. Peacefuls are potentially great leaders because of their mellow mood and innate people skills, they would prefer to be left alone and let someone else make all the decisions and do all the work. If they take over, they might offend someone or create conflict, and that is the worst case scenario for Mr. Peaceful. Whereas a powerful roommate will take charge, and try to be your boss, a peaceful roommate will make you do everything by default. Make sure he knows there are things expected of him.

Third, there is the popular personality. Mrs. Popular is the life of the party and she lives for social occasions. When Mr. Powerful is planning his next career move, and Mr. Peaceful is lounging in a beanbag, Mrs. Popular is planning the next big party and texting five people about nothing important while she does it. Mrs. Popular is great to have around because she will make any occasion fun, but she has a tendency to be immature and forgetful. If you end up living with Mrs. Popular, be patient when she doesn't act her age and constantly shows up late.

Finally, there are the people that prefer everything to be perfect. More commonly, these people are referred to as OCD types. Their clothes and hair are perfect, and their socks are neatly arranged in the drawer and organized by brand. Mrs. Perfect is great to have around because she keeps everything tidy and organized, and she never misses an appointment. However, Mrs. Perfect has a pessimistic outlook on life and can get down in the dumps very quickly, if things are not kept to her standards. If you room with Mrs. Perfect, do your best to pick up after yourself and keep things as she had them. Also, Mrs. Perfect tends to get down on herself, so look for opportunities to encourage her.

Everyone is some combination of these four personality types. By having some understanding of yourself, you can better understand others. This will pay great dividends as you live together and work through your differences. Differences between people are inevitable, so let's consider five ways to work through conflict.

First, *learn to appreciate differences.* It is true that our experiences shape who we are, but God has programmed each one of us with a unique personality. Rather than complaining about this, we need to see these differences as complements to our weaknesses. The Scriptures compare the church to a body (1 Cor 12.17–31). Each part of the body is needed. If you can learn to view your roommate as a different part of the body, rather than a pest, your relationship will improve by leaps and bounds.

Second, *learn to forgive.* At the core of Christianity is forgiveness. We must forgive others because we have been forgiven (Eph 4.32). We are continually in need of forgiveness (1 John 1.8–10). No matter how many times someone may sin against us, we must forgive (Matt 18.21–22). There will likely be times when you get upset with your roommate, but you must have a forgiving spirit. If we do not forgive others, we will not be forgiven (Mark 11.26). No matter how upset you may be, and no matter what someone has done to you, remember that God is the judge (Rom 12.19–21). It is not your job to avenge. We are to follow the example of Christ (Eph 4.32), and when it comes to forgiveness, there is no better example. He was able to say "Father, forgive them, for they do not know what they do," (Luke 23.34) of those who had just nailed his hands and feet to a cross. Learning to forgive is so important. Compassion is always better than cruelty.

Third, *treat your roommate like you want to be treated.* As the Sermon on the Mount was nearing a close, Christ said, "So whatever you wish that others would do to you, do also to them, for this the Law and the Prophets" (Matt 7.12). This is one of the most profound teachings on how to make a relationship succeed. Through the years, the "great minds" have said similar things. In fact, the "great minds" before Christ, came close to this monumental truth but missed the mark. Confucius remarked, "What you do not want others to do to you, do not do to others. Isocrates, a student of Socrates, is credited with saying, "Do not unto others what angers you if done to you by others." Do you see the difference? Many men had taught that if you do not want others to do you harm, you should not harm them. However, Christ taught that it is not enough to simply avoid harming someone. We must actively do good in the lives of others.

Fourth, *be positive about people.* There was an elderly man who used to sit in front of a store on the edge of town. One day, a man who was moving to the town rode in on his horse. "How are the people here?" the new man asked. "I'd like to ask you something," said the old, local man. "How were the people where you came from?" "Oh, they were awful," he replied. "They would cheat you, lie to you, and steal from you. There was nothing good about those people." The old man sighed. "Unfortunately, that's exactly how you will find them here."

A little while later a man came by who was moving from the same town as the previous man and he asked the same question. "How are the people here?" The old man responded the same way. "How were the people where you came from?" "They were great," he responded. "The most honest, loyal, loving people a man will find." The old man smiled. "That's exactly how you will find them here."[2] This story contains a great truth. Oftentimes, the difference is our perception of people: Do we look for their flaws or their strengths?

Fifth, *realize that you are not perfect*. Too often we hold others to a higher standard than we hold ourselves. Our lives should not convey the message, "If I make a mistake, I overlook it. If you make a mistake, I hang it over your head." Whether it's a small thing like forgetting to wash the dishes or something larger, be patient with others.

Numerous times I have criticized others, only to later do the same thing myself. I always recall an incident that happened behind the wheel. I was at a store trying to park, and a car was driving the wrong way in the parking lot. This prevented me from pulling into a space. Criticisms of this ignoramus filled my head. I looked up, and here came another one. Another vehicle driving the wrong way in this parking lot! I looked closer and suddenly I realized I was the problem. While I was busy critiquing the first driver, I had quit paying attention and made the same mistake. Now I was headed down the wrong lane, and people were upset with me.

Are you trying to convince your roommate to do things differently? A patient approach will persuade. "With patience a ruler may be persuaded, and a soft tongue will break a bone" (Prov 25.15).

Who you live with is a very important decision. Choose wisely. Whenever conflict occurs, be humble and look at yourself first. As speaker Benjamin Zander said, "Success is measured by how many people's eyes are shining around you. If the eyes of someone in my life are not shining, I need to ask myself, 'What am I doing wrong?'"

Questions for Personal Reflection or Group Study

1. Do you think it is important to live with Christians? What advantages are there? Do you see any disadvantages?

2. How would you describe your personality? If you have a roommate, how would you describe his or her personality?

3. Are there ways your roommate's personality complements your personality?

4. What are some things you find frustrating about your roommate? What are some things *you do* that annoy your roommate(s)?

5. If you are having problems with your roommate(s), what are some things you can do to improve your relationship?

Avoid Gossip

Four preachers met for a friendly gathering. During the conversation one preacher said, "People come to us and pour out their hearts, confess certain sins and needs. Let's do the same. Confession is good for the soul." In due time all agreed. One confessed he liked to go to movies and would sneak off when away from his church. The second confessed to liking to smoke and the third confessed to gambling. When it came to the fourth one, he wouldn't confess. The others pressed him saying, "Come on, we confessed ours. What is your secret or vice?" Finally he answered, "It is gossiping and I can hardly wait to get out of here!" This humorous story illustrates a painful truth. Gossip is a problem for everyone. While it is a temptation at every stage of life, it seems to rear its ugly head extra-often on college campuses.

When there are roommate problems, as discussed in the previous chapter, gossip abounds. Let's say that two people have been living together for a year. They have not followed any of the advice in the last chapter and they are on each other's last nerve. How can they make themselves feel better? Why, tell anybody who will listen all about the other person's faults of course (and exaggerate along the way). Clearly, that is not what should take place, but it happens far too often. Somehow, when we are frustrated with someone, we can easily recall everything they have done wrong in life.

The Scriptures contain many warnings about gossip. The best way to ruin a relationship is to gossip about the other person. As the wisdom of Proverbs tells us, "A dishonest man spreads strife, and a whisperer separates close friends" (Prov 16.28). Paul did not want to see the church torn apart by gossip, thus he wrote, "For I fear that perhaps when I come I may find you not as I wish, and that you may find me not as you wish—that perhaps there may be quarreling, jealousy, anger, hostility, slander, gossip, conceit, and disorder" (2 Cor 12.20). Just how serious is gossip? By no means is it a small thing. God said that those who practice it deserve to die (Rom 1.29–32).

A Christian must not have the reputation of a gossip. I am convinced that if we truly love people we will not gossip about them. When a person is gossiping about someone else, who is it on the other end? More times than not it is someone he dislikes. Therefore, to overcome gossip we must cultivate love.

"Love is patient and kind" (1 Cor 13.4). There is nothing patient or kind about gossip. Gossip is often the result of impatience, malice, and an unforgiving spirit. To resist the temptation to gossip, we must be patient with one another and "not grow weary in doing good" (2 Thess 3.13).

"Love does not envy" (1 Cor 13.4). Gossip is often the product of jealousy. People become envious because someone has something he wants or is in a situation which they would like to enjoy. Too many people have fabricated stories about others when they are green with envy. "I wonder what Mr. Smith had to do to get that job promotion," turns into, "Mr. Smith helped the boss embezzle money." "How did Mr. Davis afford that new house?" over time becomes, "Have you heard about Mr. Davis' gambling problem?" When envy strikes, false assumptions follow. Then it finally becomes full-blown gossip and slander. Galatians 5.21 warns that the envious will not inherit the Kingdom of God. Undoubtedly, envy creates division, and a primary way it does so is through gossip.

"Love does not boast" (1 Cor 13.4). Occasionally, gossip is not intended to tear down others as much as it is intended to lift ourselves up. If I can tell you something bad about somebody, suddenly I look pretty good. Pride and boasting, therefore, are sources of gossip. How many tales could have been prevented by a dose of humility? In order to have unity and brotherly love, we must be humble (1 Pet 3.8). A person in need of God's grace has no choice but to be humble (Prov 3.34).

"Love is not irritable or resentful" (1 Cor 13.5). It is difficult to gossip about someone when you love that person. However, when you resent a person, the temptation is strong. We are to love one another and love is not resentful.

"Love does not rejoice at wrongdoing" (1 Cor 13.6). When something causes us to rejoice, we talk about it. Engaged couples talk about their upcoming wedding. Newlyweds excitedly discuss their future. Proud parents will tell you more than you might want to know about their children. The list could go on and on. We talk about the things we enjoy. I am afraid too many people enjoy the mistakes of others. Why else would they talk about it? We like knowing the details of someone's demise. Perhaps we just don't hate sin enough. "Let love be genuine. Abhor what is evil; cling to what is good" (Rom 12.9). If we abhor evil, we won't broadcast it.

Quiet the Courier

When we love someone, we will help that person avoid sin. However, it is discouraging how often people will listen to gossip without intervening. If the person were engaging in some other sin, we would call them out, but for some reason gossip is treated differently. After all, we have to know these things in order to pray for someone, right? There is a huge difference between concern for a person's soul and just enjoying a juicy piece of information. James writes, "Therefore, confess *your* (italics added) sins to one another and pray for one another, that *you* (italics added) may be healed" (Jas 5.16). He did not write, "Confess *their* sins...that *they* may be healed."

Whether we like it or not, silence approves. If someone is gossiping and you quietly nod your head, you are supporting them. We must follow the teaching of Ephesians 5.11 and, "Take no part in the unfruitful works of darkness, but even expose them." Some people gossip about gossips. Quietly they go around and inform everyone of Ms. Jones' gossip problem. We must tell others so we can pray for her. How hypocritical. Let's examine ourselves and see where we can improve.

When in doubt, leave it out.
This useful advice can apply to everything from recipes to writing, but it is a phrase to remember when you think about the harm gossip can do. If you are relaying a story about someone else, and you have any doubt, leave it out. The tongue is a fire (Jas 3.6), and an unfit word can create a spark that will burn a relationship.

We ought to THINK before speaking about someone. Ask yourself if what you are going to say is:
True
Helpful
Inspiring
Necessary
Kind
Is it true? Clearly if a word is not true, it should not be spoken. Lying is something in which Christians should not engage. "Therefore, having put away falsehood, let each one of you speak the truth with his neighbor, for we are members one of another" (Eph 4.25).

Is it helpful? Is the information you are relaying helpful or hurtful? If someone would be hurt by what you say, it would be best to leave it out. Words are easier retained than retracted. In other words, you can apologize, but you can't take words back.

Is it inspiring? Does your speech inspire others or tear them down. Our words should build up not destroy. "Therefore encourage one another and build one another up, just as you are doing" (1 Thess 5.11).

Is it necessary? Some details would be better left out. For instance, I was talking to one of the members of a congregation about the budget, and he proceeded to tell me the exact dollar amount one of the families gives. In no way was this information pertinent to the discussion. If it's not necessary don't include it. The more words you speak, the more likely your tongue will slip. "When words are many, transgression is not lacking, but whoever restrains his lips is prudent" (Prov 10.19). A wise man knows when to hold his peace.

Is it kind? Unfit speech is absent in an atmosphere of kindness. "Let all bitterness and wrath and anger and clamor and slander be put away from you, along with all malice. Be kind to one another…" (Eph 4.32).

Don't take any chances. When in doubt leave it out. The following poem sums up this chapter quite well:

In the course of your conversation each and every day,
Think twice, try to be careful of what you have to say;
Your remarks may be picked up by someone's listening ear,
You may be surprised at what some people think they hear.
Things that you innocently say, or try to portray,
Can be changed, and greatly exaggerated along the way;
Many stories change for the worse as they are retold.
So try to keep any questionable remarks "on hold."
May I give all of you some very sound advice?
When you speak of others, say something nice;
Try to say good things, regardless of who is around,
If you have nothing good to say, don't utter a sound.
You may find that an innocent remark, in the end,
May lose you a close and valued friend.[1]

Questions for Personal Reflection or Group Study

1. Can you remember a time when you were the subject of gossip? How did you feel?

2. Have you found gossip to be a problem on campus? Why do you think this is?

3. What must we do to overcome this temptation?

4. Is the one listening to gossip less at fault than the one doing the talking? Discuss.

5. Currently, how do you decide what to include in a story about someone and what to leave out? What can you do to improve your criteria?

Develop a Strong Work Ethic

How many times did you hit the snooze button this morning? If you are like many college students, the number is in double digits. In college, many people have more freedom than they have ever experienced before, but with freedom, comes responsibility. You have to be self-motivated. There will probably be no one yelling at you to wake up, and most of your professors don't care if you're in class or not. Because of this, many students have become lazy, adopted the "a D is good enough" mentality, and found themselves living back home with Mom and Dad after one semester. This is a shame from an academic standpoint, but even more than that, it's not in keeping with being a Christian. The saved should not be slothful. What does the Bible say about laziness? Quite a bit. Let's first consider what the Old Testament reveals about laziness, and then what the New Testament says about our work ethic.

The Old Testament on Laziness
1. A lazy person will live in poverty.

> Go to the ant, O sluggard; consider her ways, and be wise. Without having any chief, officer, or ruler, she prepares her bread in summer and gathers her food in harvest. How long will you lie there, O sluggard? When will you arise from your sleep? A little sleep, a little slumber, a little folding of the hands to rest, and poverty will come upon you like a robber, and want like an armed man. (Prov 6.6–11)

A slack hand causes poverty, but the hand of the diligent makes rich. (Prov 10.4)

The soul of the sluggard craves and gets nothing, while the soul of the diligent is richly supplied. (Prov 13.4)

Slothfulness casts into a deep sleep, and an idle person will suffer hunger. (Prov 19.15)

The sluggard does not plow in the autumn; he will seek at harvest and have nothing. (Prov 20.4)

It is ironic that many people go to college in an attempt to become financially secure, but end up with a heap of debt and nothing to show for it. The sluggard will always be dependent on someone else. We need to make the lives of those around us blessed, not burdensome.

2. A lazy person is not dependable.

Like vinegar to the teeth and smoke to the eyes, so is the sluggard to those who send him. (Prov 10.26)

If you have a group assignment, don't count on the sluggard. If he comes at all, he will be there late and leave early. "If you want something done right, do it yourself," was a saying probably coined by someone who sent a lazy man on a mission. There are few things more irritating than relying on a sloth to get a job done. As you prepare yourself to go out into the working world, make sure your potential employer knows you are a hard worker. Not many people will hire someone with credentials that point toward laziness.

3. A lazy person has a defeatist attitude.

The way of a sluggard is like a hedge of thorns, but the path of the upright is a level highway. (Prov 15.19)

The sluggard says, "There is a lion outside! I shall be killed in the streets!" (Prov 22.13)

A slothful person thinks he will lose before he ever starts. These are the people who drop a class immediately after the syllabus is handed out. His way "is like a hedge of thorns." He can never get where he wants, because something is always in his way. What's standing between the sluggard and success? Only himself.

4. A lazy person does not take care of things.

> Whoever is slack in his work is a brother to him who destroys. (Prov 18.9)

> I passed by the field of a sluggard, by the vineyard of a man lacking sense, and behold, it was all overgrown with thorns; the ground was covered with nettles, and its stone wall was broken down. (Prov 24.30–31)

When I was younger, I cut grass during the summers for a little extra money. One of the women on the street where I lived would call me periodically to have her grass cut. Why I continued to cut her yard, I don't know. She would wait until it was about a foot high and then call. One afternoon I was mowing this woman's lawn (more like forest) and I ran over a cereal bowl. Who knows how long it had been there? Proverbs calls that type of person a sluggard.

5. A lazy person does not finish the task.

> The sluggard buries his hand in the dish and will not even bring it back to his mouth. (Prov 19.24)

Lazy students don't do assignments or write papers. Nor do they pay the bills on time. "When the going gets tough, the tough get going," does not apply to the lazy man. When the going gets tough, he goes home.

6. A lazy person has no self-discipline.

> The desire of the sluggard kills him, for his hands refuse to labor. (Prov 21.25)

A lazy person does whatever feels good, and avoids work at all costs. You can be sure that the lazy student will be out at a party the night before finals. We must not support the habits of the lazy. We read in 2 Thessalonians 3.10, "If anyone is not willing to work, let him not eat."

7. A lazy person thinks he is wise.

> The sluggard is wiser in his own eyes than seven men who can answer sensibly. (Prov 26.16)

Oftentimes the person who thinks he is really something, really has no clue. Proverbs also contains many warnings for the proud. The two often accompany each other.

The New Testament on Work Ethic
1. Our conduct should glorify God.

> So, whether you eat or drink, or whatever you do, do all to the glory of God. (1 Cor 10.31)

> And whatever you do, in word or deed, do everything in the name of the Lord Jesus, giving thanks to God the Father through him. (Col 3.17)

Whatever we do, we need to ask ourselves this question: Does my behavior glorify God? In every aspect of life, our conduct should be in keeping with God's commands. If we act slothful instead of sanctified, people will see right through the façade. I remember being shocked when the guy who sat in front of me in microeconomics came into class wearing a shirt with a religious message. I was taken aback because he was the quintessential sloth. If he mustered up the fortitude to come to class, he was thirty minutes late. Those of us who sat around each other knew one another's grades, and he had failed every test. He would come into class and boast of his parties and conquests the night before only to make 30s and 40s on his papers. Then one day, this individual paraded through campus with an evangelistic message on his shirt. Do you not think people can see the hypocrisy in that? Our conduct will either bring glory to God (Matt 5.16; 2 Pet 2.12), or it will blaspheme the name *Christian* (Jas 4.4; 2 Pet 2.10).

2. Work as though you are working for the Lord.

> Rendering service with a good will as to the Lord and not to man. (Eph 6.7)

> Whatever you do, work heartily, as for the Lord and not for men. (Col 3.23)

In no way do I mean for this to sound irreverent, but if Christ were your professor, what would you be doing differently? Would you go to class on time everyday?

Would you study harder? The fact of the matter is, we are slaves to Christ. "Likewise he who was free when called is a slave of Christ" (1 Cor 7.22). As a slave, we must do all things as though we are working for Him. He is our master, and we work for Him all day, everyday. Whether you are shopping for milk, or studying for math, you are His. Our conduct then, must glorify Him.

Questions for Personal Reflection or Group Study

1. Why do you think laziness is such a temptation in college?

2. Look back through the verses cited from Proverbs and write your own description of a lazy person.

3. What other verses or stories in the Old Testament can you find dealing with laziness/work ethic?

4. Look back through the verses cited from the New Testament and write your own description of a person with a good work ethic.

5. What other verses or stories in the New Testament can you find dealing with laziness/work ethic?

Place Membership with a Local Church

Many churches in college towns have a very loose attitude when it comes to attendance. First, they know that many students will be there for a few years at most, so membership is never stressed. Second, many students go home on the weekends so if someone is not there, it is assumed that he or she is visiting family. This is a recipe for disaster. People float in and out and no one knows who is a member and who is a visitor. Students fall through the cracks and little to no effort is made to restore them because everyone just assumes they are going home on the weekends, and maybe have a class on Wednesday night they couldn't avoid.

Is membership important?
It is true that in comparison to many topics, the Scriptures reveal little about membership in a local church. There are two passages, however, that would seem to stress the importance of having a close relationship with a local group of Christians.

In Acts 9.26, we read in regards to Paul, "when he had come to Jerusalem, he attempted to join the disciples." The Greek word translated join is *kollao*. It does not mean a casual acquaintance, but rather as Vine's notes "primarily, to glue or cement together, then, generally, to unite, to join firmly."[1] The word is used in Luke 10.11 in reference to the way dust sticks to the feet. "Even the dust of your town that clings (*kollao*) to our feet we wipe off against you. Nevertheless know this, that the kingdom of God has come near." Even more interesting, it is used to describe the bond of marriage. "Therefore a man shall leave his father and his mother and hold fast (*kollao*) to his wife, and the two shall become one flesh" (Matt 19.5). The word *kollao* is in some versions translated *cling* or *cleave*. This is what Paul wanted to do with the disciples in Jerusalem. He wanted to join. He wanted to have an intimate, family-like relationship.

In 1 Peter 5.2, elders are encouraged to "...shepherd the flock of God that is among you..." This implies that elders must know who is a part of the group. They must have knowledge of who has desired to *kollao*. This verse shows us that God places importance upon membership in a local church. How else will the elders know their sheep? By placing membership, you are helping the elders fulfill their duty to the members and to the Lord.

The Benefits of Membership

There are many benefits to placing membership with a church. First, someone will be watching out for your soul. One of the advantages of joining a local church is the oversight of elders. A proper functioning church will have a strict membership and elders who watch over the members. God has designed this structure. Take advantage of it. A primary reason people lose their faith in college is because they never place membership with a local church, and therefore, no one is actively watching out for their souls. I have heard some people say, "When I was in college I didn't live right, but there was nobody encouraging me or watching out for me." These same people never placed membership with a church. While it is the obligation of all Christians to encourage, if you don't place membership, don't be upset if no one comes calling after you. No one is aware you are a part of the congregation and want a real relationship with the church family.

Second, you will have opportunities to serve. I firmly believe that the best way to stay out of trouble is to stay busy. Idle hands are the devil's workshop. Teach a bible class, be in charge of the sound equipment, cut the grass at the church building, decorate the class rooms, prepare the communion-just do something to be involved. When you are a member, these opportunities will likely be presented to you. Take them. Do all that the church will let you. You will be too busy to engage in the things many of your peers are, and you will likely hold yourself to a higher standard. Those who gave me opportunities to preach and teach during college, played a huge role in my being faithful. Of course I sinned, but I never quit the Lord. One of the main reasons that I did not was that I knew I had to be in a pulpit somewhere on Sunday. I will be forever grateful for these opportunities.

Third, you will be included in more activities, and therefore, develop more friendships. Sometimes students complain that they are left out and not invited to events outside of services. Who are these people? You guessed it. They are the ones who never placed membership. No one has their contact information because they never identified with the group. When you become a member in a local church, you will suddenly discover that people are friendly after all. Remember, do not blame others for something that is not their fault.

Fourth, you will be accountable to these new-found friends. It is very important that you are under the elders' oversight, but it is also vital that you have friends who will hold you accountable for your choices and lifestyle. When you place membership, you will be able to serve and get to know others. Suddenly, you will have a support group. The more the merrier.

Three Groups of Students

When it comes to attending a local church, there are three types of college students: those who only come when their parents are in town, those who will come when they find the time, and those who are present each and every time. Let's examine each group and see what temptations they will face.

First, there are those who will only be seen at services when they have family in town. These are the people who put on a good show when Mom and Dad come to visit. Usually they are the people who complain that a church is unfriendly, but never stick around and talk to anyone. They say that the bible classes are boring and irrelevant, but they never prepare or take an active part in the class.

If you find yourself in this category, realize that the problem is not everyone else. Yes, perhaps certain people could be more engaging, and certain teachers could attempt to be more interesting, but you will never be happy until you adopt a servant's mindset. Quit thinking about what you should be receiving, and start thinking about what you can give. Every person has unique talents that can be used. What are yours?

If you know of someone in this first group, think of ways to encourage him or her. Make a special effort to get to know the newcomers. If you can cultivate a relationship with them outside of services, they will be more willing to be active in the church, because they have a friend there. More times than not, these people just need for someone to reach out to them. Why not be that person?

Second, there are those who come when they feel like their schedule is not too full. These people will be there occasionally on Sunday mornings, but rarely any other time. The problem is priorities. They think to themselves, "If I go to church I won't have time to study." Time management, which will be discussed in a later chapter, is at the core. Their exams are marked on their calendar, but church events are not. I always found it interesting that many of the individuals in this group have no qualms about taking a thirty minute break from studying to watch a TV show, but anything of a spiritual nature "just takes too much time."

What is most important in life? As someone once aptly said, "You never fail a class because you are a Christian." Some may argue with that statement, but I whole-heartedly agree. Personally, I always felt rejuvenated after attending services, especially around finals. A prayer would be offered, a song would be sung, a message would be spoken, and I would leave with plenty of energy to do any last minute studying. I recall a specific incident on a Wednesday night. I was worn out and stressed out from all the demands of teachers toward the end of the semester. However, on this night there was a short talk delivered on Matthew 14.29–31, the story of Peter walking on the water. The question was posed, "Why did Peter sink?" The answer of course is that he got distracted and afraid, and took his eyes off of Jesus. The point was made that when people start to "sink" in their classes or their relationships, it is never because they looked at Jesus too much. It's always because they got distracted and took their eyes off of him. They get stressed out because of exams and they feel they no longer have time to pray, and they no longer take time to read His word. Then, for some reason they become even more stressed and uptight. Its funny how that happens, isn't it? That thought still gives me encouragement today.

If finals are approaching and you feel like the only person who is still attending services, gently remind people why Peter sunk. Also, continue to feed yourself spiritually. You'll reach a level of contentment and peace that others around you will notice. "And the peace of God, which surpasses all understanding, will guard your hearts and minds through Christ Jesus" (Phil 4.7). If you go back to verse 6, you will see that prayer produces this peace.

If you are in the third category, the type of person who is there every time the doors are open, keep it up, but do not let up. "Therefore let anyone who thinks that he stands take heed lest he fall" (1 Cor 10.12). The first type of person we discussed is cold, the second type is lukewarm, and the third is hot. However, this last type of student may face a unique set of temptations. They may begin to see themselves as holier than others and adopt a self-righteous attitude. They may view others with contempt and be very judgmental. Having a laid back attitude about attendance may not be a temptation, but perhaps arrogance is. Going to a party on Saturday night may be not the least bit enticing, but they may be tempted to look down on such individuals and be apathetic about their souls.

So, in which group will you be? Are you the type of person others introduce themselves to each time you come, because you are only seen once a semester? If so, make a special effort to get involved. Are you the kind who will be there as long as it doesn't conflict with your academic and social pursuits? If you answered *yes*, then remember that times only get tougher and more stressful when Christ is pushed out of the picture. Or are you a pillar and leader who is always involved? If that describes you, then make sure to follow the wise old saying, "Never look down at someone unless you're about to pick them up."

Questions for Group Study or Personal Reflection

1. What does the Bible say about membership in a church?

2. What does 1 Peter 5.2 have to do with placing membership?

3. What to you is the most compelling benefit of membership in a church?

4. Three types of students were discussed. In your local church, which type do you think is most prevalent?

5. What can you do to encourage someone who only attends when family is in town?

6. What can you do to encourage someone who only attends when their life is not hectic?

7. What unique temptations do those face who are always present?

Be Honest

"Hey, slide your paper over a little bit," says the 6' 4", 240 pound football star. "Do you think I could see your homework?" asks the beauty queen as she bats her long eyelashes. Ever since the written test was invented there have been cheaters. It is quite frightening just how many people have been handed a diploma, who did little or no work themselves. I read a story not too long ago about a weatherman who forged his way to the top. He had no credentials, but he convinced everyone in his path that he was a competent meteorologist. The man predicted the weather on the nightly news of a major television station without the foggiest idea of what the weather would do. Many people graduate having never written a paper or taken a test themselves. How should a Christian respond to the idea that, "It's ok as long as you don't get caught."

Cheating is Lying

It's plain and simple. Cut and dried. A cheater is a person who misrepresents himself and the truth, and consequently is a liar. Whether you copy someone's test, write the formulas on your hand, or let your girlfriend write your papers, you are lying. Therefore, to see what God says about cheating we must understand what has been revealed in Scripture about lying.

A righteous person is characterized as being a person who hates dishonesty. "The righteous hates falsehood, but the wicked brings shame and disgrace" (Prov 13.5). The book of Zephaniah describes God's people as being people of truth. "But I will leave in your midst a people humble and lowly. They shall seek refuge in the name of the Lord, those who are left in Israel; they shall do no injustice and speak no lies, nor shall there be found in their mouth a deceitful tongue. For they shall graze and lie down, and none shall make them afraid" (Zeph 3.12–13).

On the other hand, Scripture tells us that those who lie are wicked in the Lord's eyes. "Your tongue plots destruction, like a sharp razor, you worker of deceit. You love evil more than good, and lying more than speaking what is right" (Psa 52.2–3). In Hosea 4.1–2, lying is mentioned alongside murder. "Hear the word of the Lord, O children of Israel, for the Lord has a controversy with the inhabitants of the land. There is no faithfulness or steadfast love, and no knowledge of God in the land; there is swearing, lying, murder, stealing, and committing adultery; they break all bounds, and bloodshed follows bloodshed." Lying is said to be something in which Christians no longer engage. "Do not lie to one another, seeing that you have put off the old self with its practices" (Col 3.9).

Lying is not a new sin. The Bible is full of stories about people who succumbed to the temptation of lying or being deceitful. Eve (Gen 3), Cain (Gen 4), Jacob (Gen 27), Joseph's brothers (Gen 37), and Peter (Matt 26) are just a few examples. These accounts are given for our learning that we might avoid making the same mistakes. We must be honest. The consequences of doing otherwise are serious.

In Genesis 3, the devil who is the father of all lies (John 8.44), told Eve she could eat of the fruit of a tree that God had strictly placed off-limits (Gen 3.4–5). Rather than confront her wrongdoing, Eve attempted to hide and cover it up

(Gen 3.7–13). Sin came into the world by means of deception. Adam and Eve were punished for their sin, and mankind still feels the consequence of this sin today (Gen 3.15–19).

One chapter further, in Genesis 4, Cain killed his brother Abel (Gen 4.8). God asked Cain where Abel was and Cain flat-out lied. He said, "I do not know" (Gen 4.9). God never lets a liar go without being punished. Cain was told that we would be, "a fugitive and a wanderer on the earth" (Gen 4.12).

By the time Jacob came on the scene, lying was still a problem. He and his mother, Rebekah, contrived a plan to deceive his father, Isaac. Before his brother Esau left to go hunting, Isaac told Esau to bring him back some tasty food and he would be blessed. Rebekah overheard this and convinced Jacob to pretend he was Esau. He put skins on his hands and neck (Esau was a hairy man), and took Isaac a bowl of food. Isaac thought Jacob was Esau. So, he blessed Jacob. This put a great strain on Jacob and Esau's relationship. "Now Esau hated Jacob because of the blessing with which his father had blessed him" (Gen 27.41).

The sons of Jacob sold their brother, Joseph, into slavery. They took Joseph's robe, dipped it in blood, and told their father that Joseph had been killed by a wild animal (Gen 37.29–35). Not only was it wrong of the brothers to have done this, it caused their father much grief.

Although Peter was a great man, at one point in his life he was a liar. Peter was a close friend of Jesus, but he denied ever knowing Him. Not once, not twice, but three times (Matt 26.69–75). Imagine the regret and guilt that Peter must have experienced. Lying leads to lamenting.

God has never taken lying lightly. First and foremost, those who live a lying lifestyle will not be in Heaven. "But as for the cowardly, the faithless, the detestable, as for murderers, the sexually immoral, sorcerers, idolaters, and all liars, their portion will be in the lake that burns with fire and sulfur, which is the second death" (Rev 21.8). In Acts 5.1–11,

Ananias and Saphira were found guilty of lying and they were struck dead. The liar will not be able to escape from God. "A false witness will not go unpunished, and he who breathes out lies will not escape" (Prov 19.5).

Is it really worth it? Cheating is very serious. If the possibility of getting kicked out of school does not motivate you, forfeiting your salvation should. Think twice before turning in work that is not yours.

Partners in Crime

Clearly, cheating is wrong, but what if you help someone else cheat? You are just doing good to everyone (Gal 6.10) right? Much the same as with gossip, we cannot aid someone in doing wrong. What would you think of a person who lent someone a gun so he could commit murder? Obviously the owner of the gun is not innocent. He is a partner in crime. When you let someone cheat, or do his work for him, you are essentially enabling him to do wrong.

The pages of the Bible make this very clear. "Blessed is the man who makes the Lord his trust, who does not turn to the proud, to those who go astray after a lie!" (Prov 40.4). "No one who practices deceit shall dwell in my house; no one who utters lies shall continue before my eyes" (Psa 101.7). Not only should we shun lying, we should pray that God will keep us far from deceitful situations. "Put false ways far from me and graciously teach me your law!" (Psa 119.29).

When you help someone cheat, you are setting her up for disappointment and struggles later in life. Not long ago I read about a father who wrote his son's English papers from high school all through graduate school. Has this father helped his child? No, he has crippled him. Similar things have happened in math classes. Even if people graduate with honors, but they can not add or subtract well enough to manage their own finances, you have prepared them for a lifetime of failure.

Cheating Yourself

It is true that if you aid others in cheating, you are setting them up to fail. Therefore, if *you* cheat, what have you done? You have set *yourself* up to fail. Cheating can be detrimental to your soul because cheating is lying, but cheating can also be detrimental to your own education and development. If you cheat, you do not learn the necessary skills to be successful in your field of study.

I remember a specific time when cheating was a temptation for me in a high school keyboarding class. I sat next to a good friend who was a great typist. She was always the first done with her work. This class was at the end of the day and right after gym. Rarely did I want to sit at a computer and type, especially numbers. I hated typing numbers. I was so slow. So, I got a great idea one day. Why not let my friend do it for me? It ended up being an awful idea. To this day, I still cannot type numbers. Sure, I can poke them with my index finger, but I cannot type them. You know what? I wish I could. But that's what cheating does. You cheat yourself and later you will wish you had not.

There is also the potential of doing great harm to others. Now, what if I were a nurse or doctor who had cheated my way through school? Would you want me to be your doctor? What if I were an accountant or lawyer who had cheated through school? Would you want me to represent you? Cheaters in the school leave with the potential to do great harm, even kill people. Don't cheat.

Questions for Personal Reflection or Group Study

1. Why is cheating a temptation?

2. From your own experience, what percentage of people do you think cheat?

3. The stories in the Bible are recorded for our learning. What are some lessons you can learn from those who lied?

4. Have you ever "helped" someone by letting them cheat? Would you do anything differently today?

5. Can you remember a time when you stifled your own growth by cheating? Would you do anything differently today?

Part Three

The Battle of Sinful Surroundings

The Battle of Sinful Surroundings

Sin is rampant on college campuses. You must be prepared to engage in the battle of sinful surroundings. In high school, the temptations are there, but the majority of young people are still living with Mom and Dad. And even if Mom and Dad are really lenient, high school students are too young to go everywhere they want, and too young to buy everything they want. This changes in college. No longer are the guardians around, and now everyone is old enough to legally go wherever and do whatever. And if you're not, you have a friend that is. To some, this is the ticket to freedom and they take a one-way trip into the world. On top of that, many college students do not work long hours, so they feel like they have plenty of time to experiment with everything that was off limits before. In this section, we will look at the two most prevalent sins on college campuses, and what the Spirit has revealed about each.

Don't Pick Up the Bottle

Recent surveys and polls have found the following facts about college students and drinking: [1]

- 72 percent of college students report that they used alcohol at least once within the last 30 days. Within the last year, 84 percent of students report they drank alcohol.

- Among college students under the age of 21, 82 percent report using alcohol within the past year and 69 percent report using alcohol within the last 30 days.

- 78 percent of college athletes report that they used alcohol on at least one occasion in the past 30 days. Within the past year, 88 percent of student athletes report using alcohol.

- One in five athletes believe other students' drinking adversely affects their involvement on an athletic team or in other organized groups.

- Student athletes are more often the heaviest drinkers in the overall student population. Half of college athletes (57 percent of men and 48 percent of women) are binge drinkers, and experience a greater number of alcohol-related harms than other students. College athletes are also more likely than other students to say that getting drunk is an important reason for drinking.

- 86 percent of college students involved in fraternities and sororities, report that they used alcohol on at least one occasion in the past 30 days prior to completing the survey. Within the past year, 93 percent of Greeks report using alcohol.

- An overwhelming majority of college students feel drinking is a central part of the social life of both fraternities and sororities (79 percent and 72 percent, respectively). Specifically, Greek-involved students feel drinking is a central part of the social life in fraternities (88 percent) and sororities (78 percent).

- 67 percent of college freshmen report that they used alcohol on at least one occasion in the past 30 days. Moreover, eight out of ten freshmen report using alcohol within the past year.

- On average, college freshmen report they drink more than five drinks per week (5.7 drinks). 45 percent of college freshmen report they engaged in binge drinking at least once during the two weeks prior to completing the study.

- One-third of freshmen students report their alcohol use has increased within the past 12 months.

- Freshmen students who began drinking and/or reported being drunk before 16 years of age were more likely than other freshmen to binge drink in college.

- On average, female college students drink almost four drinks per week compared to their male peers who drink nine drinks per week.

- Overall, 35 percent of college females report their alcohol use has remained about the same over the past 12 months and 22 percent that their alcohol use has increased over the past year. By comparison, 33 percent of female freshmen report their alcohol use has increased and 26 percent report their use has remained about the same over the past 12 months.

- According to the 2001 Harvard School of Public Health College Alcohol Study (CAS), about three out of ten college students drove after drinking. Study results also indicate drinking and driving increases in direct proportion to binge drinking. 58 percent of frequent binge drinkers, 40 percent of occasional binge drinkers, and 19 percent of non-binge drinkers reported they drove after drinking

- According to the National Highway Traffic Safety Administration (NHTSA), young drivers are over-represented in both alcohol and non-alcohol traffic related fatality rates. Alcohol-related traffic fatality rates are nearly twice as great for 18, 19, and 20 year olds as for the population over 21.

Percent of Students Who Report They Used Alcohol in the Past 30 Days and Past Year		
Student Groups	Past 30 Days	Past Year
All Students	72%	84%
Under 21	69%	82%
Athletes	78%	88%
Greeks	86%	93%
Freshmen	67%	80%
Female Students	71%	85%

Anyone who says drinking is not a problem on college campuses has his head buried in the sand. The drinking game *beer pong* is proof. There is now the World Series of Beer Pong (affectionately referred to as the WSOBP) where the winner receives $50,000. Based on my own observations, alcohol is the number one reason college students quit the faith. They want to drink, but they know it will put them at odds with other Christians. Therefore, they have a decision to make. They can either put down the bottle, or let Satan win the battle. Sadly, many have and will choose foolishly.

Clearly, it is a sin to get drunk (Rom 13.13; Gal 5.19–21; 1 Cor 6.9–10; 1 Pet 4.3), but the argument is often made that the Bible never condemns the use of alcohol, only drunkenness. Therefore, people reason it's ok to go to a party and have a few as long as you don't end up being the town drunk. Let's open up the Bible and see what we can learn about this important topic. First, we will look at the times drinking is mentioned in a negative context, then we will consider those passages which speak of it positively, finally we will provide a biblical answer to the question, "Should a Christian drink?"

More times than not, when the Scriptures mention alcohol, its use is condemned. The following is a list of things that alcohol causes:

- *Staggering* – "they reeled and staggered like drunken men and were at their wits' end" (Psa 107.27).

- *Poor judgment* – "These also reel with wine and stagger with strong drink; the priest and the prophet reel with strong drink, they are swallowed by wine, they stagger with strong drink, they reel in vision, they stumble in giving judgment" (Isa 28.7). "…whoredom, wine, and new wine, which take away the understanding" (Hos 4.11).

- *Loss of modesty* – "Noah began to be a man of the soil, and he planted a vineyard. He drank of the wine and became drunk and lay uncovered in his tent. And Ham, the father of Canaan, saw the nakedness of his father and told his two brothers outside. Then Shem and Japheth took a garment, laid it on both their shoulders, and walked backward and covered the nakedness of their father. Their faces were turned backward, and they did not see their father's nakedness" (Gen 9.20–23).

- *Sexual immorality* – "'Come, let us make our father drink wine, and we will lie with him, that we may preserve offspring from our father.' So they made their father drink wine that night. And the firstborn went in and lay with her father. He did not know when she lay down or when she arose. The next day, the firstborn said to the younger, 'Behold, I lay last night with my father. Let us make him drink wine tonight also. Then you go in and lie with him, that we may preserve offspring from our father.' So they made their father drink wine that night also. And the younger arose and lay with him, and he did not know when she lay down or when she arose. Thus both the daughters of Lot became pregnant by their father" (Gen 19.32–36).

- *Anger and fighting* – "Wine is a mocker, strong drink a brawler, and whoever is led astray by it is not wise" (Prov 20.1). "Who has woe? Who has sorrow? Who has strife? Who has complaining? Who has wounds without cause? Who has redness of eyes?" (Prov 23.29).

God has always advised religious leaders to stay away from intoxicating drinks. In Leviticus 10.8–9, God directly told Aaron, "Drink no wine or strong drink, you or your sons with you, when you go into the tent of meeting, lest you die. It shall be a statute forever throughout your generations.'" Kings were also cautioned against its use. "It is not for kings, O Lemuel, it is not for kings to drink wine, or for rulers to take strong drink, lest they drink and forget what has been decreed and pervert the rights of all the afflicted" (Prov 31.4–5). In the New Testament, an elder is not to be "a drunkard" (1 Tim 3.3).

Without a doubt, the Scriptures condemn drunkenness and warn us of the consequences, but what about all the passages that mention wine in a positive way? Let's consider the following ways that wine is presented.

- *A gift from God* – "You cause the grass to grow for the livestock and plants for man to cultivate, that he may bring forth food from the earth and wine to gladden the heart of man, oil to make his face shine and bread to strengthen man's heart" (Psa 104.14–15).

- "And she did not know that it was I who gave her the grain, the wine, and the oil, and who lavished on her silver and gold, which they used for Baal" (Hos 2.8).

- "Wisdom has built her house; she has hewn her seven pillars. She has slaughtered her beasts; she has mixed her wine; she has also set her table" (Prov 9.2).

- "Come, everyone who thirsts, come to the waters; and he who has no money, come, buy and eat! Come, buy wine and milk without money and without price" (Isa 55.1).

- "I came to my garden, my sister, my bride, I gathered my myrrh with my spice, I ate my honeycomb with my honey, I drank my wine with my milk. Eat, friends, drink, and be drunk with love!" (Song 5.1).

- "Go, eat your bread with joy, and drink your wine with a merry heart, for God has already approved what you do" (Ecc 9.7).

- *Used by Christ for a miracle* – "On the third day there was a wedding at Cana in Galilee, and the mother of Jesus was there. Jesus also was invited to the wedding with his disciples. When the wine ran out, the mother of Jesus said to him, 'They have no wine.' And Jesus said to her, 'Woman, what does this have to do with me? My hour has not yet come.' His mother said to the servants, 'Do whatever he tells you.' Now there were six stone water jars there for the Jewish rites of purification, each holding twenty or thirty gallons. Jesus said to the servants, 'Fill the jars with water.' And they filled them up to the brim. And he said to them, 'Now draw some out and take it to the master of the feast.' So they took it. When the master of the feast tasted the water now become wine, and did not know where it came from (though the servants who had drawn the water knew), the master of the feast called the bridegroom, and said to him, 'Everyone serves the good wine first, and when people have drunk freely, then the poor wine. But you have kept the good wine until now.' This, the first of his signs, Jesus did at Cana in Galilee, and manifested his glory. And his disciples believed in him" (John 2.1–11).

- *Used for medicinal purposes* – "No longer drink only water, but use a little wine for the sake of your stomach and your frequent ailments" (1 Tim 5.23).

How do we reconcile these two uses of what seem to be alcoholic beverages? At times, drinking is condemned. Other times, it is condoned. How do we make sense of this? Granted, it is a difficult topic. Instead of doing a word study or comparing biblical drinks to 21st century drinks let's look at three simple, basic reasons that a Christian should not drink.

Drinking alcohol hurts your *influence*.

First, you will lose your influence with those of the world. Some people hold the belief that drinking alcohol will make them "just one of the guys" and will give them an opportunity to influence the lost. Actually, the opposite is true. When one of your non-Christian friends sees you drink, you will likely lose whatever influence you had. Why? Because most people in the world do not associate Christians with drinking. They think of Christians who drink as being hypocrites. Whether we like it or not, the world has certain expectations of us. This should be taken into account. For instance, a Christian is to guard his speech. No specific words are categorized as "bad words" in the Bible. So, how do we determine what combination of letters makes a "bad word"? Society has deemed certain words unacceptable. The words are different depending on culture, custom, and country. When a Christian says one of these words, the first thought that pops into the mind of the unsaved is, "I didn't think Christians said that."

I want to make myself very clear so that there will be no misunderstanding or misrepresentation of what I have written. The world does not determine what we can and cannot do. However, when the world acknowledges that an activity is not in keeping with the behavior of a Christian, should we engage in that activity? Surely not. After all, it was Jesus who reminded His disciples, "Behold, I am sending you out as sheep in the midst of wolves, so be wise as serpents and innocent as doves" (Matt 10.16). It can take a long time to build trust in someone and influence them for good. Are you willing to throw that away for a drink? I hope not.

Second, you will lose your influence with those of the church. As I have written previously, many people quit the faith because they would rather drink than maintain a good relationship with other Christians. One way we lose our influence with brethren is by doing something that offends them or causes them to stumble. Romans 12.10 tells us to "Love one another with brotherly affection. Outdo one another in showing honor." In Romans 14, Paul presents a scenario where love would be lacking. In those times, there were some who thought that meat should not be eaten, and Paul writes that if he was to eat meat he would be lacking in love (Rom 14.15). In Romans 14.21, we read, "It is good not to eat meat or drink wine or do anything that causes your brother to stumble" (Rom 14.21). Christ spoke about the seriousness of making someone stumble: "But whoever causes one of these little ones who believe in me to sin, it would be better for him to have a great millstone fastened around his neck and to be drowned in the depth of the sea" (Matt 18.6). In Romans 12.18 we read, "If possible, so far as it depends on you, live peaceably with all."

Even if in your mind you can somehow scripturally justify social drinking, it will put you at odds with other Christians. You will no longer be living peaceably with all. If it is up to you, you should live peaceably. Drinking is not an involuntary behavior, it is a choice. A very poor choice.

Before you decide to drink, ask yourself two questions: Would this make me look hypocritical? Would this offend my fellow Christians? I have yet to meet an American college student in the 21st century who can answer *no* to both of those questions.

Drinking alcohol lowers your *inhibitions*.
I have heard countless stories of people doing things they regretted when they drank. A person does not have to be sloppy drunk to have a change in behavior. Especially if a person has not built up a tolerance to the drug, just a little bit can result in altered conduct. I was told by a friend that he liked to have a little bit of alcohol at a party because he

was usually shy, and it helped him become willing to dance. Alcohol, even a small amount, can aid people in doing things they usually would not.

Ephesians 6.11 encourages us to "Put on the whole armor of God, that you may be able to stand against the schemes of the devil." Each drink puts a chink in the armor. When a person is full-blown drunk, the armor is off. Each sip prior to this makes the armor weaker and weaker. I do not know about you, but I need my armor to be as strong as possible.

Drinking alcohol is *illegal* if you are under 21.
This is a point that is probably not discussed as much as it should be. If you are under 21, which the majority of college students are, there is no way you can honestly justify drinking. Why? Because you are breaking the law. We are citizens of Heaven, but while we are here we must obey the laws of the land (Prov 24.21; Matt 17.25–27; Rom 13.7). It is interesting that even immoral lawmakers realize that some people should not be drinking.

Alcohol is by far the number one tool Satan uses on college campuses. Before you decide to drink, ask yourself why you want to do so. Do you need to relax? Maybe your prayer life isn't what it should be. Do you think it will make you happy? You need to reevaluate your source of joy (Phil 4.4–7). Do you want to change your personality? If so, you are saying God is a bad Creator. Do you want to fit in? If we are not standing out, then something is wrong. A Christian is to be a round peg in a world of square holes.

Questions for Personal Reflection or Group Study
1. Why do you think so many people choose to drink?

2. Based on your observation, what percentage of college students do you think drink regularly?

3. According to the Old Testament, what does alcohol cause?

4. How can drinking alcohol cause you to lose your influence?

5. List other reasons why a Christian should not drink. Think of as many as you can.

Wait

Three sentences forever ring in my ears. They are three sentences that revealed the mentality regarding sex during the college years. Each is six words that showed the world's view of sex.

The first was, "Don't forget to take your pill." I was hanging out with a couple of girls that I assumed were not the party type. Actually, I thought they were just the opposite of that. One of them had turned into a good friend. Her boyfriend was coming over and her roommate gave her the friendly, yet subtle, reminder. My curious look and her guilty expression answered my unasked question. I remember feeling extremely disappointed. I was not romantically interested. It's just that I thought she was living up to a higher standard.

The second came a year later. "I've decided to end my sexcapade," she said in a frightened voice across the cafeteria table. I considered her an acquaintance. She lived on the female side of the dorm, and had developed quite a reputation. Basically, her goal was to have sex with as many guys in the dorm as she could. On this day, she thought she might be pregnant and that fear caused her to say those six words that are forever etched in my brain.

The third memorable statement occurred two years later on a stormy night. The electricity had been knocked out by the inclement weather. Therefore, many people were gathered in the parking lot of the apartment complex. As I walked by the crowd on the way to my apartment, I overheard a girl say something to the effect of, "We met at a sex party." She was referring to someone that had been brought up in the conversation.

Unfortunately, many Christians have gone off to college only to find themselves muttering similar sentences by the end of the semester. In this chapter, we will look at what the Spirit has revealed about this topic, and then we will discuss some ways to avoid succumbing to this temptation.

God's Word

In the book of Genesis, we clearly see that God intended for a man and a woman to be together. Since the beginning, this was God's design. "Therefore a man shall leave his father and his mother and hold fast to his wife, and they shall become one flesh" (Gen 2.24). This simple statement rules out homosexuality, premarital sex, and extramarital affairs. Marriage is the designated place for the sexual relationship.

"Let marriage be held in honor among all, and let the marriage bed be undefiled..." (Heb 13.4). This union has been created by God, and is a beautiful thing when understood correctly. Many people leave God out of the picture all together. They are of the persuasion, "It is my body, and I'll do with it what I want!" God has not left the punishment of such unrepentant individuals to speculation. He has been very clear. Those who live a sexually immoral lifestyle will not be in Heaven.

> Or do you not know that the unrighteous will not inherit the kingdom of God? Do not be deceived: neither the sexually immoral, nor idolaters, nor adulterers, nor men who practice homosexuality, nor thieves, nor the greedy, nor drunkards, nor revilers, nor swindlers will inherit the kingdom of God. (1 Cor 6.9–10)

Now the works of the flesh are evident: sexual immorality, impurity, sensuality, idolatry, sorcery, enmity, strife,
jealousy, fits of anger, rivalries, dissensions, divisions, envy,
drunkenness, orgies, and things like these. I warn you, as I
warned you before, that those who do such things will not
inherit the kingdom of God. (Gal 5.19–21)

For you may be sure of this, that everyone who is sexually
immoral or impure, or who is covetous (that is, an idola-
ter), has no inheritance in the kingdom of Christ and God.
(Eph 5.5)

Let marriage be held in honor among all, and let the marriage bed be undefiled, for God will judge the sexually immoral and adulterous. (Heb 13.4)

But as for the cowardly, the faithless, the detestable, as for
murderers, the sexually immoral, sorcerers, idolaters, and
all liars, their portion will be in the lake that burns with
fire and sulfur, which is the second death. (Rev 21.8)

Outside are the dogs and sorcerers and the sexually immoral and murderers and idolaters, and everyone who loves
and practices falsehood. (Rev 22.15)

Some people practice abstinence because of the risk of
unplanned pregnancy or STDs. While it is good that people
are abstaining, these should not be the first reasons given as
to why. The ultimate reason is that God's law forbids a sexual
relationship outside of marriage.

Why has God warned us against this? There must be a
reason. He is not just trying to take the fun out of life. The
reason is that unlawful sexual activity results in the break-
down of society's basic unit, the family. Clearly homosexuality destroys the family. Adultery does as well. A lax view of
fornication has caused some to never get married, and has
caused others to not appreciate the institution of marriage.
God has given us boundaries for a reason. Stay within them,
and be rewarded.

Your Plan

Famous painter, Pablo Picasso, once said, "Our goals can only be reached through a vehicle of a plan, in which we must fervently believe, and upon which we must vigorously act. There is no other route to success." In order to overcome sexual temptation, you must have a plan. Otherwise, you will find yourself in the same pool of regret over and over again.

A close friend of mine, after realizing that this area was a strong temptation for him, decided to develop his plan. He decided he would not kiss a woman again until after he said, "I do." Was it extreme in the eyes of some? Yes. Did it work? Yes. Everyone's plan may differ, but a good plan should include the following three things:

The Person. Who are you going to date? A better question would be, *what type of person* are you going to date? Ask yourself this, "Will this person help me abstain?" If the answer is *no*, you need to reconsider. I am not saying you should never date a non-Christian. What I am saying is that if you choose to, with hopes of converting them, you need to make your standards known in the beginning. If they are not respectful of your convictions then you should move on. Sometimes, a Christian will date someone who has no moral compass when it comes to sex. What is even worse is that they never discuss it. If you do this, you set yourself up for failure.

Even if you are dating a Christian, you should discuss "the line." And then stay far from it. It should go without saying that there are sinful sexual activities other than intercourse. However, couples may not agree on where "the line" is. It should probably be more conservative than where most set it. Jesus said that "Everyone who looks at a woman with lustful intent has already committed adultery with her in his heart" (Matt 5.17). Remember this verse when you discuss what is "too far."

The Place. Where do you spend most of your time? Your answer may determine whether or not you will win this battle. Your strategy should include the places you will and will not frequent. If you are like many college couples I know, you probably spend much of your time as a couple somewhere alone in front of the TV. While I do think that you need to spend some time alone with a person to truly know them, these times should not be in the majority. Hang out in groups. This should be a surefire way to overcome the snares of Satan.

The Point in Time. When are you with the person in the place you have selected? I know that college students keep crazy hours, so this may not apply to some. For the majority of people, however, the later it is, the stronger the temptation. Satan may not tempt you at three in the afternoon, but he will at three in the morning. If you are up late studying together, go to a library or a coffee shop. If you can not find one open, find a 24-hour restaurant. It may not be the best atmosphere, but it sure beats Hell fire.

The Point of Your Conversation

What do you talk about? If you are not careful, sexual innuendos will fill the void in your conversation. First, this is not the type of speech that characterizes a Christian. "But sexual immorality and all impurity or covetousness must not even be named among you, as is proper among saints. Let there be no filthiness nor foolish talk nor crude joking, which are out of place, but instead let there be thanksgiving" (Eph 5.3–4). It is interesting that the Spirit inspired Paul to write about speech in a context regarding sexual immorality. Second, talking about it will only make it more difficult to say *no*. Homer Hailey once said that he avoided sexual sin by just not dwelling on it. That is part of a good plan. Remember, what you talk about, shows what you think about. What you think about is, more times than not, what you will end up doing.

God's Word is very clear when it comes to sexual relationships. It is something to be shared only by a heterosexual, married couple. If someone lives a lifestyle not in keeping with this command, he cannot expect to be in Heaven. The way to avoid this sin is to develop a plan. Planning prevents problems.

Questions for Personal Reflection or Group Study

1. How would you describe the mentality of most people your age, that you know, regarding sexual activity?

2. List some reasons (spiritual, psychological, and physical) why one should wait until marriage. Try to think of some reasons not even mentioned in the chapter. There are several.

3. Do you think having a plan is important? Why or why not?

4. Do you currently have a plan? If so, what is it? If not, what should it include?

5. Why does the person matter? The place? The time? Your conversation?

Part Four

The Battle of Stewardship

The Battle of Stewardship

The parable of the talents (Matt 26.14–30) teaches a valuable lesson. God expects us to manage the resources He has given us. Whether it be our time, our money, or our abilities, we must be responsible. As Christ said to two of the servants in the parable, "Well done, good and faithful servant. You have been faithful over a little; I will set you over much" (Matt 26.21, 23).

Many students have fallen victim to the battle of stewardship. They don't manage their time well, and they don't manage their money well. Therefore, they end up feeling overwhelmed to the point that their faith becomes secondary.

Learning to be a good steward is vital in life. During the college years, you will likely experience more freedom than ever before. A Christian must be responsible with this freedom. By doing so, you are showing God that you can handle what you have been given.

Be Responsible with Your Money

The average American is deep in debt, lives paycheck to paycheck, and will never truly retire. Although spending habits and money management are learned at a young age, the college years are when most people set the tone for the rest of their life. Ramen noodles are still a best seller in college towns, which means that a large portion of students are attempting to live within their means. However, there are just as many students running up a heap of debt on credit cards, taking out monstrous student loans, and driving this year's make and model. Eventually, it catches up to them. If you think college is stressful, talk to someone who lived beyond her means during college. The stress of finals pales in comparison to the stress of paying back all the debt that has piled up. The wisdom of Proverbs states: "The borrower is the servant to the lender" (Prov 22.7). In this chapter, we will discover what the Bible says about the proper view of money, how it should be used, and clear up some misconceptions. This is one battle you cannot afford to lose…literally.

The View of Money

What is the wrong view of money? Simply put, the wrong view is to think it is ours. Those who think they have become financially stable without God's help will begin to think, "I earned it, so I can spend it how I want." This thinking leads to a selfish lifestyle. God is thrown out of the picture, and money is viewed as a right, rather than a blessing. God keeps your heart beating, your feet moving, and your mind working. Any talent we possess that can be used for financial gain has been given to us by Him. "And you shall remember the Lord your God, for it is He who gives you power to get wealth, that He may establish His covenant which He swore to your fathers, as it is this day" (Deut 8.18).

Those who think they are in powerful positions would do well to remember the answer to the questions posed in Isaiah 40.

> Do you not know? Do you not hear? Has it not been told you from the beginning? Have you not understood from the foundations of the earth? It is he who sits above the circle of the earth, and its inhabitants are like grasshoppers; who stretches out the heavens like a curtain, and spreads them like a tent to dwell in; who brings princes to nothing, and makes the rulers of the earth as emptiness. Scarcely are they planted, scarcely sown, scarcely has their stem taken root in the earth, when he blows on them, and they wither, and the tempest carries them off like stubble. (Isa 40.21–24)

The richest, most powerful person is nothing more than a grasshopper. We should recall this when we start thinking that what we have is ours.

So, what is the right view of money? It is a gift from God. When you view your finances as a blessing rather than a right, your whole outlook will change. Your focus will shift from the rat race to God's grace. A proper view of money is the first step in managing it well. Instead of, "This is mine so I'll do with it as I please," our attitude should be, "God has given this to me, so how can I give back to him?"

The Use of Money

What does the Bible tell us about the use of money? First, let's look at how it should not be used. The Scriptures clearly teach that money should not be hoarded. "Do not lay up for yourselves treasures on earth, where moth and rust destroy and where thieves break in and steal, but lay up for yourselves treasures in heaven, where neither moth nor rust destroys and where thieves do not break in and steal" (Matt 6.19–20). A similar warning is given in the book of James: "Come now, you rich, weep and howl for the miseries that are coming upon you. Your riches have rotted and your garments are moth-eaten. Your gold and silver have corroded, and their corrosion will be evidence against you and will eat your flesh like fire. You have laid up treasure in the last days" (Jas 5.1–3). We will not be judged based on our finances, but rather on our faith. Therefore, riches won't help us on that day. "Riches do not profit in the day of wrath, but righteousness delivers from death" (Prov 11.4). "See the man who would not make God his refuge, but trusted in the abundance of his riches and sought refuge in his own destruction" (Psa 52.7).

People hoard the things they love. If you don't believe it, just watch the overly dramatic A&E show, *Hoarders*. Why would a woman have forty cats? Because she loves her feline friends. So it is with money. It is a commodity the world loves. Paul warned against this in 1 Timothy 6.10: "For the love of money is a root of all kinds of evils. It is through this craving that some have wandered away from the faith and pierced themselves with many pangs."

Money should not be hoarded. It should be given. We read in Matthew 6.20 that we should "lay up...treasures in heaven..." Similar phraseology is used in Scripture as a reference to giving. "Sell your possessions, and give to the needy. Provide yourselves with moneybags that do not grow old, with a treasure in the heavens that does not fail, where no thief approaches and no moth destroys" (Luke 12.33). "And Jesus, looking at him, loved him, and said to him, 'You lack one thing: go, sell all that you have and give to the poor, and you will have treasure in heaven; and come, follow me'"

(Mark 10.21). "They are to do good, to be rich in good works, to be generous and ready to share, thus storing up treasure for themselves as a good foundation for the future, so that they may take hold of that which is truly life" (1 Tim 6.19–20). X marks the spot. Is your X on heaven or earth?

One way we can give is by giving to the church. We have the example in 1 Corinthians 16.2. "On the first day of every week, each of you is to put something aside and store it up, as he may prosper, so that there will be no collecting when I come." We should give out of joy. "Each one must give as he has decided in his heart, not reluctantly or under compulsion, for God loves a cheerful giver" (2 Cor 9.7). Giving does not stop at church, it starts there. There are multiple ways to give. You can give to those who are needy (although as a college student you may feel like the needy one). You can also give of your time, your energy, and your talents. Find ways to give back. Be creative.

Clearing up Misconceptions

Is it wrong to save? Some have reached the conclusion that a Christian should not save, and by doing so, he is greedy or hoarding. This idea is not in keeping with Scripture. Saving is part of being a good steward. Joseph encouraged Pharaoh to store up grain for the coming famine. "And let them gather all the food of these good years that are coming and store up grain under the authority of Pharaoh for food in the cities, and let them keep it. That food shall be a reserve for the land against the seven years of famine that are to occur in the land of Egypt, so that the land may not perish through the famine" (Gen 41.35). The book of Proverbs teaches that the wise man saves. "Precious treasure and oil are in a wise man's dwelling, but a foolish man devours it" (Prov 21.20). "He who tills his land will have plenty of bread, but he who follows frivolity will have poverty enough" (Prov 28.19). Saving for the future is not wretched. It is wise.

Can a Christian be wealthy and faithful? The answer is *yes*. It is true that riches make righteous living difficult. "And again I say to you, it is easier for a camel to go through the eye of a needle than for a rich man to enter the kingdom of God" (Matt 19.24). However, we must keep in mind that Paul did not write that *money* is the root of evil, but that the *love of money* is the root of evil (1 Tim 6.10). Some people have gone as far as to say that the poorer a man is, the more righteous he must be. Such individuals must never have read the Old Testament. "In the house of the righteous there is much treasure, but trouble befalls the income of the wicked" (Prov 15.6). There are countless examples of people who were righteous and rich. Job illustrates the point. "There was a man in the land of Uz whose name was Job, and that man was blameless and upright, one who feared God and turned away from evil. There were born to him seven sons and three daughters. He possessed 7,000 sheep, 3,000 camels, 500 yoke of oxen, and 500 female donkeys, and very many servants, so that this man was the greatest of all the people of the east" (Job 1.1). To say that a righteous person will not accumulate wealth is to misunderstand the subject of money altogether.

Use Some Sense, Keep Your Cents

Finally, just don't be stupid. Opening up a credit card account and racking up charges so that you can have a free slice of pizza on campus is not very bright. Buying nine gallons of milk because the tenth is free is pretty dumb unless you are planning on making milkshakes for the whole dorm. Companies prey heavily upon college students because they have learned that it is easy to make a buck off of gullible kids. You are an adult now. Act like one.

Do not let your money tell you where to go. Tell it where to go. View your money as a gift, not an entitlement. When you do this, you will be more apt to give, and less tempted to hoard. There is nothing immoral about being wealthy. In fact, the more you have, the more you can give. Just never allow your finances to destroy your faith. If you develop the right view of money and use it the right way now, you will be in a position to bless others down the road.

Questions for Personal Reflection or Group Study

1. What type of spending habits do most of the students you know have?

2. What is the incorrect view of money? The correct view?

3. What is the incorrect way to use money? The correct way?

4. How is a person's view of money connected to her use of money?

5. What do the Scriptures teach about saving and accumulating wealth?

Be Responsible with Your Time

"I just don't have enough time to do everything." I've found that a simple way to determine whether or not someone is a college student is to see how many times they utter the aforementioned phrase. If you are a student who takes classes seriously, you will likely be swamped. On top of that, if you work a job your time is even more limited. Throw in a few social activities and you will be stretched thin. Add a boyfriend or girlfriend to the equation and life gets extra busy (if you are a guy, expensive too). Oh yeah, and don't forget to sleep. The recommended time is eight hours a night. This will help energize the batteries for another stressful day.

How well people manage their time will dictate how successful they are in their classes, their faith, and their future. Poor time management will lead to failing class, falling away spiritually, and a difficult road ahead. On the other hand, if you manage your time well, you will be able to reach your goals. In this chapter we will discuss the importance of setting goals and their role in time management.

Goal Setting 101

The road to success in college has three checkpoints: aspiration, visualization, and perspiration. You must aspire to do something. Once you know what you want to accomplish, you then must visualize *how* you will do it. After you have done that, it is just a matter of getting it done. For example, if you haven't already, you will decide your major (aspiration). Then, you will have to choose your classes and perhaps your emphasis (visualization). Next, you must attend those classes and study hard (perspiration).

Goals are bite-sized visions. A goal is the road connecting visualization and perspiration. Without aspiration, you will never have a vision. Without a vision, you will never have a goal. And without a goal you will have nothing to work toward.

Goals are the driving force behind success. As Zig Ziglar said: "If you aim at nothing, you'll hit it every time." If you have no idea what you want to achieve, you will not achieve anything. J.C. Penney remarked, "Give me a stock clerk with a goal, and I will give you a man who will make history. Give me a man without a goal, and I will give you a stock clerk."

In order for your goals to produce positive change, they must comprise seven areas (in no particular order): spiritual, social, academic, financial, health, career, and family. Furthermore, goals that work must be five things. First, *goals must be specific*. If a business says, "We want to be successful," that's not a goal, that's an aspiration. If they say, "We want to be successful by raising profits," that's still not a goal, that's a vision. If they say, "We want to be successful by raising profits five percent," *voila*! Now, you have a goal. If a student says, "I want to make a good grade," that's an aspiration. If she says, "I want to make a good grade by studying for tests," that's a vision. If she says, "I want to make a good grade by studying for tests, thereby, making at least a B on all my assignments," now we have a goal.

A specific goal is a measurable goal. That's number two. *Goals must be measurable*. Someone who says, "I want to draw closer to God," has made a good, yet somewhat unquantifiable statement. However, if that same person says, "I want to draw closer to God by reading my Bible for 20 minutes a day," we suddenly have a specific goal which is measurable. Every day, she can determine whether or not she made steps in the right direction.

Third, *goals must be individualistic.* In other words, they must be yours. I cannot set a goal for you, and you cannot set a goal for me. Your goals must be just that, yours and yours alone. Just like your faith must be your own, whatever goals you set to build that faith must be yours.

Fourth, *goals must have a time limit.* For example, reading through the Bible in a year is a common goal. That seems like a big task. Therefore, people become overwhelmed and quit or never even start. If you can break a task into smaller time increments, it will seem much more doable. There are 1,189 chapters in the Bible. By dividing this by 52 (weeks in the year) you arrive at 23. You must read 23 chapters a week to read the Bible in a year. That doesn't sound too overwhelming, but if it does, make it even smaller. 1,189 divided by 365 (days in the year) equals 3.25. Now, that seems very achievable. Some days read three chapters, other days read four chapters, and you'll read the Bible through in a year.

Fifth, *goals must be in writing.* Determine your specific, measurable, individualistic, time constrained goal, and put it in writing. Put it in a place you are forced to look. You will constantly be reminded.

When you feel like you don't have enough time to do everything, review your goals. If an activity helps you accomplish your goal in that area, do it. If not, avoid it. For instance, you may have the social goal of getting to know everyone at church. Getting on Facebook 20 times a day is a social activity, but that probably won't help you get to know everybody at church. If it does not help you achieve your goal, do something else.

We have already mentioned that the seven areas of goal setting should be spiritual, social, academic, financial, health, career, and family. Now, place these in order of importance. Which is most important, which is least important? Hopefully, spiritual is first. Since you are in college, academic should be high on the list. Other than that, your list will likely depend on your interests, your background, and your personality. I played a sport at the collegiate level for two years, and even after that I enjoyed being active. *Health*, therefore, was high on my list. I will confess that it was at times too high. That is just an example to show that what you value and what you are involved in will likely determine your order. Just remember, no matter what, *spiritual* should always be first. "But seek first the kingdom of God and His righteousness, and all these things shall be added to you" (Matt 6.33).

Now that you have numbered your seven areas, draw four boxes. Label these boxes *necessity*, *important*, *deception*, and *discard*. When you have a lot on your plate, pull out your list of priorities and your four boxes and begin to fill them up.

For example, let's consider the priority *academic*. Suppose you are taking four classes: a history, a math, a language, and a science. Now, let's consider hypothetically what you have coming up in each. We will say that you have a writing assignment due next week in history, a major exam in Math this week, a reading assignment for class discussion in language later in the month, and a small lab report at the end of the semester summarizing your science class. Now, start filling in your boxes. Math would go under *necessity;* history will likely be in number two, *important*; your language class will go in *deception*. We label box three *deception* because whatever goes there always tries to deceive you into thinking it's of number one importance, especially if it is an area in which you have procrastinated. Even if you have been guilty of this, you have a math test in a few days, so put it on the back burner for now. Science will go into *discard*. It's not due for months, and it won't take very long if you do a little here and a little there throughout the semester.

Now you have your four boxes labeled. For your math exam, decide what part you really need to study most, and begin sorting again. Many exams will cover three or four concepts, so you can likely repeat the process. Which area do you need to study the most? If it is a math, what type of problems or theorems are the most difficult for you? This should probably go in *necessity*. Will there be material that you have already mastered? If so, put it in *discard*. You may want to review, but don't spend the majority of time on something you already understand well. By going through this simple process, you can determine what is worthy of your time and what is not.

The challenge comes when you have obligations to fulfill in different areas. This is where people make mistakes and get into trouble. For example, as we have previously discussed, they will neglect to worship because they feel they have to study for an exam. Let's make up another example. Suppose its Wednesday night (spiritual), and you have a big assignment due on Friday (academic). There is also an intramural sporting event on Thursday (health/social) and you need to work a few more hours before you can pay the bills on your apartment (financial). How do you determine what to do when? From personal observation I would say that many people would skip church on Wednesday to work, go to the game on Thursday, then throw the assignment together at the last minute. They have missed out on a time to worship, and likely made a poor grade. All of these things could have been done, and done well if they would have pulled out their priority list. Spiritual is first, so Wednesday night service goes into *necessity*. Although the team needs you, the intramural game isn't as important as the other two so it goes into *discard*. Your current grades and budget will determine what goes in boxes two and three. A little forethought will go a long way to helping you accomplish what you want, keep your sanity, and most importantly, serve the Lord. [1]

Having a goal will help you determine what is and what isn't important in a given area. Furthermore, placing these areas and your goals for each in order of importance will help you determine which activities to take part in and which to cast off. By doing this you will be able to manage your time more efficiently. If you kill time, time will end up killing you.

Questions for Personal Reflection or Group Study

1. What percentage of students, would you say, struggle with time management?

2. In what areas should we set goals? Can you find any verses in the Bible that deal with these areas and how we should view them?

3. In order for a goal to be effective and motivating, what five things must it be?

4. When you consider Matthew 6.33, "seek first the kingdom of God" What area do you think most college students seek first? Why?

5. Do you have difficulty managing your time? If so, what can you do to improve?

Final Thoughts

In years past, academia and spirituality were virtually inseparable. A cursory reading of university history will reveal that, in many instances, society viewed the most educated as the most spiritual and vice-versa. The reason for this is simple. The university was a place to learn, not only about academics, but about God. How times have changed! Today, if colleges want spiritual scholars they have to seek them out intentionally. Schools that do so are those whose primary purpose, along with academics, is to create an atmosphere of spiritual growth. There is that word again, *purpose*. A plan will never come to fruition without it, a goal will never be met without it, and people will never succeed without it.

There you have it, the 12 tactics to keep the enemy at bay. When your science professor tells you there is no God, point to the sky, the sea, or the ground you stand on. Either one will do. When your history professor insist Jesus was, at best, a good man. Ask him to explain the empty tomb. When your philosophy teacher is adamant that the Bible is just another book, remember the process of its copying, the people who relayed the message, and the power contained therein. When your roommate gets on your last nerve, remember all the socks you have left in the floor, or perhaps all the annoying notes you have left reminding him to not leave his socks in the floor. When gossip comes your way don't just let it go in one ear and out the other because it usually gets lodged somewhere in the brain during the process. Rather, just say you are not interested. When you want to hit that snooze button just one more time remember the old cliché maxim-if you snooze you lose. If becoming involved in a local church just doesn't seem important, remember what really is important. When you are tempted to cheat instead of study, remember that when you cheat you cheat yourself. When that drink looks like so much fun, remember the pile of puke the guy across the street slept in last night. When you find yourself tempted, or perhaps pressured, to sin sexually, remember that all good things are worth waiting for. When the debts keep piling up, remember to quit piling up debt (that's pretty simple). And when there just never seems to be enough time, remember that every day has the same amount of hours. The difference is how you manage them.

The next few years of your life will be some of the most challenging, but they will also be some of the most rewarding. Always keep in mind that you are not on your own. God will hold you in His hand (John 10.28), His Son will be with you (Matt 28.20), and the Spirit will guide your steps (Psa 119.105). It is a temptation for the older generation to believe that the future is dark and dreary. Prove them wrong. *You* are the future, and the future can be as bright as you want it to be. Good luck.

Notes

Chapter 1

1. Walter Kidney, ed. 1993. *Webster's 21ˢᵗ Century Dictionary of the English Language* (Nashville: Thomas Nelson Publishers).

2. Lee Strobel, *The Case for a Creator* (Grand Rapids: Zondervan, 2004), 80.

3. Strobel, *CC*, 81.

4. Percival Davis and Dean Kenyon, *Of Pandas and People: The Central Question of Biological Origins* (Dallas: Haughton Publishing Company, 2ⁿᵈ ed, 2004), 11.

5. William A. Dembski and James M. Kushiner, *Signs of Intelligence* (Grand Rapids: Brazos, 2001), 44, quoted in Strobel, *CC*, 22.

6. Phillip E. Johnson, quoted in *World*, July/August 2002, quoted in Stobel, *CC*, 23.

7. Gordy Slack. "A Good Life." *UCI Journal*, Spring 2010, quoted in Strobel, *CC*, 23.

8. John H. Campbell and J. William Schopf, *Creative Evolution?!* (Boston: Jones and Bartlett, 1994), 4–5, quoted in Strobel, *CC*, 23.

9. Davis and Kenyon, *PP*, 9.

10. Creation Science Association of British Columbia. 2011. Darwin's Favourite Evidence: *Fraudulant*! http://www.creationbc.org/index.php?option=com_content&view=article&id=78&Itemid=62

11. Davis and Kenyon, *PP*, 2–3.

12. Richard Dawkins, "On Debating Religion," *The Nullifidian*, December 1994, quoted in Strobel, *CC*, 21.

13. "Iconoclast of the Century: Charles Darwin (1809–1882)." *Time*, December 31, 1999, quoted in Strobel, *CC*, 24.

14. Philip E. Johnson, *Darwin on Trial* (Downers Grove: Intervarsity Press, 2nd ed, 1993), 126–127, quoted in Strobel, *CC*, 16.

15. Strobel, *CC*, 43.

16. Ibid., 46.

17. Ibid., 48.

18. Ibid., 39.

19. Ibid., 54.

20. Ibid., 88.

21. Ibid., 107.

22. Ibid., 107.

23. Ibid., 106.

24. Ibid., 99.

25. Ibid., 239.

Chapter 2

1. Stanley Lawrence Glade, ed. 1963, *Cambridge History of the Bible* (New York: Cambridge University Press), 30, quoted in Josh McDowell, The New Evidence That Demands a Verdict, (Nashville: Thomas Nelson Publishers, 1999), 47.

2. Neil R. Lightfoot, *How We Got the Bible* (Abilene: ACU Press, 1986), 17.

3. Bruce M. Metzger, *The Text of the New Testament*, (New York: Oxford University Press, 1968), 9 in McDowell, NEDV, 19.

4. Norman L. Geisler and William E. Nix, *A General Introduction to the Bible*, (Chicago: Moody Press, 1968), 210, quoted in McDowell, NEDV, 21.

5. Lightfoot, *HWGB*, 66.

6. Geisler and Nix, *GIB*, 277, quoted in McDowell, *NEDV*, 23.

7. Justin Martyr, "Apology," in *Ante-Nicene Fathers*, ed. Alexander

Roberts and James Donaldson (Grand Rapids: Eerdmans, 1989), First Apology 1.67 quoted in McDowell, *NEDV*, 24.

8. Athanasius, "Letters," in *A Select Library of the Nicene and Post-Nicene Fathers of the Christian Church*, ed. Phillip Schaff (New York: The Christian Literature Company, 1888), 552, in McDowell, *NEDV*, 24.

9. Lightfoot, *HWGB*, 76–81.

10. McDowell, *NEDV*, 34.

11. John W. Montgomery, *History and Christianity* (Downers Grove: Intervarsity Press, 1971), 29, quoted in McDowell, *NEDV*, 35.

12. Frederick G. Kenyon, *Handbook to the Textual Criticism of the New Testament*, (London: Macmillan and Company, 1901), 4, quoted in McDowell, *NEDV*, 35.

13. McDowell, NEDV, 55.

14. Nelson Glueck, *Rivers in the Desert: History of Negev* (New York: Farrar, Straus, and Cadahy, 1959), 31, quoted in McDowell, *NEDV*, 89.

15. Lightfoot, *HWGB*, 37–38, 94.16. McDowell, *NEDV*, 47.

Chapter 3

1. Tacitus, "Annals," in *Great Books of the Western World*, ed. Robert Maynard Hutchins (Chicago: William Benton, 1952), 44, quoted in McDowell, *NEDV*, 121.

2. Lucian of Samosata. "Death of Pegrine," in *The Works of Lucian of Samosata*, trans. H.W. Fowler and F.G. Fowler (Oxford: The Clarendon Press, 1949), 11–13, quoted in McDowell, NEDV, 121.

3. McDowell, *NEDV*, 121.

4. Ibid., 122.

5. Flavius Josephus, *Jewish Antiquities* (Cambridge: Harvard University Press, 1963) XVIII, 33.

6. Ibid., XX, 9.

7. I. Howard Marshall, *I Believe in the Historical Jesus* (Grand Rapids: Eerdmans, 1977), 24, quoted in McDowell, *NEDV*, 135.

8. Philip Schaff, *The Person of Christ* (New York: American Tract Society, 1913) 94–95, quoted in McDowell, *NEDV*, 160.

9. Peter Kreeft and Ronald K. Tacelli, *Fundamentals of the Faith: Essays in Christian Apologetics* (San Francisco: Ignatius Press, 1993), 60–61, quoted in McDowell, *NEDV*, 161.

10. J.T.Fisher and L.S. Hawley, *A Few Buttons Missing* (Philadelphia: Lippincott, 1951), 273, quoted in McDowell, *NEDV*, 162.

11. McDowell, *NEDV*, 163.

12. Peter W. Stoner, *Science Speaks* (Chicago: Moody Press, 1963), 100–107, quoted in McDowell, *NEDV*, 193.

13. William Lane Craig, *Knowing the Truth about the Resurrection* (Ann Arbor: Servant Books, 1988), 116–117, quoted in McDowell, *NEDV*, 205.

14. Merrill C. Tenney, *The Reality of the Resurrection* (Chicago: Moody Press, 1963), 119, quoted in McDowell, *NEDV*, 268.

Chapter 4

1. Florence Littauer, *Pesonality Plus*, (Grand Rapids: Revell, 1983).

2. John Maxwell, *Winning with People Workbook*, (Nashville: Nelson Impact, 2005).

Chapter 5

1. Taken from www.sermonillustrations.com/a-z/g/gossip.htm.

Chapter 7

1. W.E. Vine, *An Expository Dictionary of New Testament Words* (Old Tappan: Fleming H. Revell Company, 1966), 276.

Chapter 8

1. Taken from www.alcohol101plus.org/downloads/CollegeStudents.pdf.

Chapter 12

1. Much of this information is taken from Dave Ramsey's *Entre-Leadership* seminar.

Also for the Graduate

Daybreak
A Guide to Overcoming Temptation
Nathan Ward

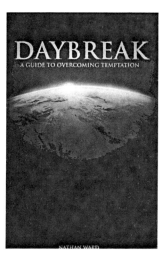

The sun rose on Jacob after his wrestling match with God. A new day dawned and he had a new name to match his new life. A similar call for daybreak is made for Christians today: come out of the darkness and into God's marvelous light (1 Pet 2.9).

As Christians, we must not live in the night. We have experienced our own daybreak and should walk in the light—but far too often, we find the darkness alluring. Daybreak examines the call to overcome temptation, a closer look at the enemy, and some practical principles for winning the battle with sin. 108 pages. $8.99 (PB).

Hard Core: Defeating Sexual Temptation with a Superior Satisfaction
Jason Hardin

So many—men and women included—are being slaughtered in their struggle with sexual sin. Individual lives, marriages, children, influences for good, ministries of gospel preachers, and entire congregations of the Lord's people are being seriously impacted. If we are going to win this battle, we must strike at the root of the problem. We must sound the call for righteous warfare. We must dedicate ourselves to hardcore holiness and fight sexual temptation with a superior satisfaction. 106 pages. $7.99 (PB).

Invitation to a Spiritual Revolution
Paul Earnhart

Few preachers have studied the Sermon on the Mount as intensively or spoken on its contents so frequently and effectively as the author of this work. His excellent and very readable written analysis appeared first as a series of articles in Christianity Magazine. By popular demand it is here offered in one volume so that it can be more easily preserved, circulated, read, reread and made available to those who would not otherwise have access to it. Foreword by Sewell Hall. 173 pages. $9.99 (PB).

Prepared to Answer: A Guide to Christian Evidences
Robert van de Weghe

Follow the personal odyssey of a man of science as he journeys from skepticism to faith. Logic, science, and history become bridges instead of barriers, as doubt is transformed into confidence. Scrutinize the evidence that compels the verdict that Christian faith rests upon truth and fact, not legend and myth. 450 pages. $7.99 (PB).

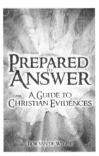

In the Garden with God
Dene Ward

Dene Ward and her husband Keith have gardened for nearly 40 years, which has shown her why God's prophets and preachers, including Jesus, used so many references to plants and planting—it's only natural. Join her for a walk in the garden with God. 142 pages. $9.99 (PB).

Built by the Lord: A Study of the Family
Edwin Crozier

A biblical and challenging look at the Lord-built home. *Built by the Lord* answers questions about the purpose of the Lord-built home, the roles in the Lord-built home, the goals of the Lord-built home, the habits a Lord-built home maintains, and how the Lord-built home interacts with the Lord's family. Each chapter comes packed with Biblically-based teaching, challenging personal responses, points for further meditation, and prayers to seed your own prayer life inviting God to build your home. 226 pages. $13.99 (PB).

For a full listing of DeWard Publishing Company books, visit our website:

www.deward.com

CPSIA information can be obtained
at www.ICGtesting.com
Printed in the USA
LVOW07s0951200817
545693LV00001B/33/P